Cambridge Student Guide

Shakespeare

Macbeth

Stephen Siddall

Series Editor: Rex Gibson

PUBLISHED BY THE PRESS SYNDICATE OF THE UNIVERSITY OF CAMBRIDGE
The Pitt Building, Trumpington Street, Cambridge, United Kingdom

CAMBRIDGE UNIVERSITY PRESS
The Edinburgh Building, Cambridge CB2 2RU, UK
40 West 20th Street, New York, NY 10011–4211, USA
477 Williamstown Road, Port Melbourne, VIC 3207, Australia
Ruiz de Alarcón 13, 28014 Madrid, Spain
Dock House, The Waterfront, Cape Town 8001, South Africa

http://www.cambridge.org

First published 2002
Reprinted 2003

Printed in the United Kingdom at the University Press, Cambridge

Typeface Scala 9.5/12pt.   *System* QuarkXPress®

A catalogue record for this book is available from the British Library

ISBN 0 521 00826 3 paperback

Cover image: © Getty Images/PhotoDisc

Contents

Introduction	**4**
Commentary	**5**
Contexts	**62**
What did Shakespeare write?	62
What did Shakespeare read?	63
Drama: the influence of genre	65
Miracle plays	65
Morality plays	66
Tragedy	67
Masque	69
What was Shakespeare's England like?	69
Witchcraft	70
Women	73
Prophecy	74
The succession to the throne	76
The divine right of kings	79
Language	**80**
Imagery	80
Antithesis	85
Soliloquy	86
Lists	87
Repetition	88
Verse and prose	89
Critical approaches	**91**
Traditional criticism	91
Modern criticism	97
Political criticism	97
Feminist criticism	100
Performance criticism	102
Psychoanalytic criticism	106
Postmodern criticism	107
Organising your responses	**109**
Writing about an extract	109
Writing an essay	116
Writing about character	120
Resources	**125**
Books	125
Films	128
Macbeth on the Web	128

Introduction

Macbeth, a leading Scottish general, has just rescued his country from the combined threats of invasion and civil war. On his return home with a fellow general 'in the day of success', he meets three strange outcasts, who describe themselves as 'the weïrd sisters' and who prophesy that Macbeth will become king. Strongly urged by his wife, he decides to 'catch the nearest way': he murders King Duncan and usurps the throne.

His reign, the rest of his life and the whole of Scotland are filled with fear and horror as Macbeth tries to secure himself and his position. Challenges come from other noblemen and from within his own conscience. His wife suffers a mental breakdown and Macbeth himself is finally defeated and killed by an army raised in England and led by the murdered king's elder son.

As a story of appalling crime and retribution, the play is unusual in giving greater focus to the tormented criminals than to their victims. Audiences generally feel ambivalent: they totally condemn the crimes but are drawn deeply into the mind of the hero/criminal. Many critics believe that the play is Shakespeare's most compelling study of the nature of evil.

Perhaps because of this intensity, *Macbeth* has a unique reputation in the theatre. Actors are superstitious about naming the play or quoting from it. It is euphemistically referred to as 'the Scottish play' and has a history of misfortune and strange events attached to productions of it. The play includes prophecy, black magic rituals, unnatural events and mental disorder. *Macbeth* is the shortest of Shakespeare's tragedies, it has no sub-plot and is often played without an interval in order to emphasise the pace and compression of its action.

The story of Macbeth is based on events in remote eleventh-century Scotland and critics have argued that Shakespeare was writing in response to concerns around 1603 when the Scottish King James succeeded Elizabeth on the English throne. Yet these particular historical origins have not made the play feel remote from contemporary audiences. It is constantly performed worldwide and has universal appeal because of the way Shakespeare dramatises corruptible human nature and Macbeth's tragic fall from greatness to catastrophe.

Commentary

Act 1 Scene 1

The play begins ominously with thunder and lightning. Three witches seem to be at the end of a meeting and preparing for their next. They refer to Macbeth, whom they intend to meet. As soon as they mention his name, they hear voices, which they address as 'Graymalkin' and 'Paddock'. Jacobean audiences believed in the superstition that witches worked through familiars, creatures such as cats and toads. The final rhyming couplet feels like a ritual that 'celebrates' some strange and ugly proceeding:

> Fair is foul, and foul is fair,
> Hover through the fog and filthy air. *(lines 12–13)*

Some critics believe that Shakespeare never wrote an opening more puzzlingly elusive than this. The scene contains questions, to which the answers are briefly factual, giving no sense of wider purposes or context. The location is uncertain and the next meeting place sounds strange and empty – 'Upon the heath.' Some productions set the scene on a deserted battlefield and show the witches scavenging for equipment and body parts as trophies and ingredients for their black magic charms.

Though the scene may feel strangely undeveloped in content, its style is simple, crisp and decisive. The Witches speak in the rhyming tetrameters of children's verse. The greatest apparent certainty is reserved for the ending: 'Fair is foul', and – as if to reinforce the point, or ensure its completeness – 'foul is fair'. Noble values of goodness and beauty are reversed in the threatening and confused atmosphere of 'fog and filthy air'. In this brief opening scene Shakespeare provides hardly any narrative, but creates a worrying vacuum in which evil can flourish.

Act 1 Scene 2

The action shifts from the supernatural world of Scene 1 to the human world. King Duncan demands information about the battle. A wounded Captain tells of recent success, of how a rebel, 'The merciless

Macdonald', was violently defeated in single combat by the loyal military hero, Macbeth. The Captain's storytelling not only informs the king, but is also a brisk dramatic device for giving narrative background to the audience.

Where Scene 1 seemed to withhold information about Macbeth, Scene 2 compensates. He is again the central absent figure, but this time presented in elaborate language. The Captain, covered in blood, lists images of blood and destruction to celebrate the hero's triumph. He speaks of swimmers, ironically destroyed by their efforts to survive, of a rebel's villainies multiplying, of Fortune smiling like a whore, of a tailor cutting a garment, an image which describes Macbeth slicing a body from the navel to the chin. The Captain seems to revel not only in how a loyal general crushed rebellion, but also in the physical business of bloodshed. There is a hectic enthusiasm in his speech, which suggests how near Scotland came to disaster and Macbeth's almost single-handed role in its rescue.

Duncan expresses approval and the Captain continues with his news. On the same day a further battle was fought against an invading Norwegian army, supported by another traitor, the Thane of Cawdor. Shakespeare has here manipulated history to suit his dramatic purposes by compressing two separate battles into a single day.

Duncan barely has time to praise the Captain when there is further news. Ross arrives and Lennox comments, 'What a haste looks through his eyes!' The speed of the storytelling conveys the speed of Macbeth's final efforts: his victory over the Norwegians and the immediate capitulation of their king, who has paid a large sum of money in compensation.

Duncan's response is immediate: he orders that the treacherous Thane of Cawdor be executed and that Macbeth be rewarded with his title. The scene ends with two sets of rhyming lines, which convey a clinching finality to the day's work, to the decisions made and to Duncan's belief that after warfare there can be a swift return to an ordered world:

DUNCAN   Go pronounce his present death
        And with his former title greet Macbeth.
ROSS I'll see it done.
DUNCAN What he hath lost, noble Macbeth hath won.   *(lines 64–7)*

Act 1 Scene 3

'. . . Macbeth hath won.' Duncan celebrated Macbeth with these words at the end of Scene 2. Now, on the heath, the Witches will do likewise, but more elaborately and obliquely. As they wait for him to arrive, one of them tells the story of a sailor who went to Aleppo, whilst his wife remained at home. The Witch visits her and, in revenge for the woman's abusive language, she will pursue the husband. When she reaches him, the Witch promises:

> And like a rat without a tail,
> I'll do, I'll do, and I'll do. *(lines 8–9)*

In Shakespeare's time, the rat was an emblem of uncontrolled lust, and 'do' was often a euphemism for sexual intercourse. Witches were thought able to inhibit a man's sexual potency, and so here the Witch intends to use sex as a weapon to destroy her victim. Many productions give these lines a malicious intensity, with the Witch stabbing a tiny figure of the victim. The other Witches participate eagerly and the leader promises that the sailor will 'dwindle, peak, and pine': he will linger in a living death.

There is no stated connection between this story and what follows: Macbeth's arrival. But in both cases the wife remains at home while the husband has been on a journey, and in both cases the Witches are eager for the encounter. As one shows her grotesque trophy of 'a pilot's thumb', the sound of a drum urges them into ritualised language and action. They conclude a charm and prepare to welcome the hero. The Witches call themselves 'The weïrd sisters' (see page 72). They perform 'hand in hand', chanting words that suggest an intricate ceremony:

> Thrice to thine, and thrice to mine,
> And thrice again, to make up nine. *(lines 33–4)*

Macbeth is returning to King Duncan to receive thanks for heroic achievement. But his first words, 'So foul and fair a day I have not seen', echo the Witches' chant in Scene 1. They suggest conflicting thoughts in a successful man who should feel secure and certain. Banquo, his fellow-general, is clearly puzzled by the Witches: his first speech begins with urgent questions and he struggles to interpret what he sees:

> How far is't called to Forres? What are these,
> So withered and so wild in their attire,
> That look not like th'inhabitants o'th' earth,
> And yet are on't? – Live you, or are you aught
> That man may question? *(lines 37–41)*

In contrast, the Witches speak with ceremonial certainty. They welcome Macbeth as Thane of Glamis, which he is, and then reach into what seems like an impossible future when they greet him successively as Thane of Cawdor and king. Macbeth makes no reply, but Banquo notices the sudden effect the words have on him:

> Good sir, why do you start and seem to fear
> Things that do sound so fair? *(lines 49–50)*

'Fear' and 'fair' are near-opposites in their meaning, but are brought together by their half-rhyme, so emphasising Macbeth's confusion. Many critics point to these lines to suggest that he already has within him the seeds of ambition and the Witches have startled him by expressing what he had hoped were private thoughts. In Banquo's words, Macbeth seems 'rapt' or entranced, implying 'wrapped' in a world of his own. Banquo demands to know what the Witches predict for him, making his request in careful and measured language. The Witches reply with three brief paradoxes:

FIRST WITCH Lesser than Macbeth, and greater.
SECOND WITCH Not so happy, yet much happier.
THIRD WITCH Thou shalt get kings, though thou be none.

(lines 63–5)

The Witches' neat antithetical language masks the confusion it expresses. Macbeth and Banquo seem to be mocked and manipulated, not just by the uncertainty of their futures, but by the elusive nature of the language itself. Macbeth recovers from his trance and makes urgent demands for more information. At this, the Witches vanish.

As the two men struggle to understand what they have seen, Ross and Angus bring news. Ross reports how the king heard of Macbeth's heroism and declared him Thane of Cawdor. Macbeth is puzzled because Cawdor lives. Angus is uncertain how Cawdor's treachery was planned, but declares with certainty that he has confessed his treason and has been stripped of his title.

In an aside, Macbeth's thoughts are drawn from Glamis and Cawdor to the prophecy that he will become king, but he refers evasively to the prospect – 'The greatest is behind' – perhaps because he has a superstitious fear of naming it. When he speaks to Banquo, he appears to be solicitous about his friend's future: 'Do you not hope your children shall be kings . . .?' Banquo declines to answer, but seems to treat Macbeth's question as a cue to give his opinion about the kingship. Again he refers to the strangeness of the situation, but seems now to be moving from puzzlement to moral anxiety, when he speaks of how devious are the agents of wickedness (the Witches):

> The instruments of darkness tell us truths;
> Win us with honest trifles, to betray's
> In deepest consequence.   *(lines 123–5)*

Neither man seems willing to speak openly. In any case, there is no time to develop any policy beyond Banquo's brief warning before he moves away to talk with Ross and Angus. Macbeth, left alone, tries to sort out his troubled thoughts in his first soliloquy of the play. It begins with performance imagery from the theatre ('prologues' and 'act'). His language inflates from 'truth' to 'happy prologues' to 'swelling' to 'imperial theme'. But his apparent confidence cannot be maintained. As he tries to unravel the meaning of what he and Banquo have heard, he is drawn into self-defeating antithesis ('ill'/'good'):

> This supernatural soliciting
> Cannot be ill, cannot be good. If ill,
> Why hath it given me earnest of success,
> Commencing in a truth?   *(lines 129–32)*

In his confusion he reaches out for certainties: there is the factual 'I am Thane of Cawdor', then his statement of what he feels to be a psychological truth: 'Present fears / Are less than horrible imaginings.' But these 'horrible imaginings' distort the mind so completely that he eventually reaches the chaotic perception that 'nothing is, / But what is not'.

The critic L C Knights describes 'the sickening see-saw rhythm' of Macbeth's soliloquy, which conveys the impression of a wildly searching mind. Shakespeare is not simply expressing a formal antithesis of good and evil as abstract ideas, such as can be found in morality plays (see page 66). He explores basic moral opposites by going deep within the hero's mind and its struggles. In this first soliloquy Macbeth only lightly alludes to murder, which he describes as 'fantastical'. The speech explores his own process of thinking, revealing that guilt, worry and the strange fascination with what is forbidden all prevent his reaching a clear conclusion. 'Smothered in surmise' is a telling image, with its implications that Macbeth's imagination is so densely packed that action is inhibited.

Banquo again uses 'rapt' to remark on Macbeth's self-absorption. Some productions suggest that Banquo is completely unaware of Macbeth's state of mind: others have him speak the line jokingly in an attempt to mask his anxiety. Macbeth drags himself into a conventionally gracious apology, but speaks perhaps more truthfully than he intends: 'My dull brain was wrought / With things forgotten.' As all four leave, he makes a tentative proposal to Banquo:

> Think upon what hath chanced and at more time,
> The interim having weighed it, let us speak
> Our free hearts each to other.   *(lines 152–4)*

'Free', meaning frank or honest, is impossible in a relationship that is becoming wary. But Macbeth needs to be clear about Banquo's attitudes. As he probes and tests, hoping for complicity, he is beginning a process which will increasingly push the two former friends apart.

Act 1 Scene 4

The scene begins with Duncan hearing of Cawdor's death. The king plays a central and confident role now, and in most productions his appearance is distinctive. He is often shown as white-bearded and a little infirm, so that the younger soldiers who surround him have to put aside their tough military roles and show gentle care for him. Some critics idealise Duncan as a king who humanises relationships with his subjects: for example, his words about Cawdor's treachery will appear full of personal regret, unlike Angus' more curt summary in the previous scene.

Malcolm's report of how the Thane of Cawdor died celebrates a sense of honour in the traitor's final moments. A less subtle play would not seek to accord respect to the criminal, but *Macbeth* consistently avoids dealing reductively with the moral absolutes of good and evil.

Macbeth, the new and trusted Thane of Cawdor, enters and so interrupts the discussion of the former, treacherous thane. Some productions reinforce the irony of the moment by having Macbeth enter early enough to overhear that Cawdor threw away 'the dearest thing he owed / As 'twere a careless trifle'. He may also hear Duncan comment that 'There's no art / To find the mind's construction in the face.' Such ironies emphasise for the audience that Macbeth knows that no one onstage, least of all the king, has any idea of the evil intentions forming in his mind.

The centre of this scene is filled with Duncan's gratitude. His language makes the duties of king and subjects feel like warm personal impulses. He weeps for joy at the loyalty he is rewarding, he embraces Macbeth and Banquo and eventually declares Malcolm to be the heir apparent with the title 'The Prince of Cumberland'. Productions which idealise Duncan play his rich language as sincerely heartfelt. Other interpretations which see Duncan as a devious operator suggest that his appointment of Malcolm is a sign that he wishes to establish his own political dynasty (see page 99). Duncan further honours Macbeth by offering himself as house guest, to which Macbeth manages a gracious response.

As the king and his court prepare to leave for Inverness, the scene ends by echoing the contrast at the end of Scene 3: a mixture of private soliloquy and public action. This time the pace is even more rapid. Macbeth has just six lines of soliloquy before he leaves. Dismayed by Malcolm's elevation to Prince of Cumberland, he calls for total darkness to conceal his malign intentions, not just from the world but even from his own consciousness:

> Stars, hide your fires,
> Let not light see my black and deep desires,
> The eye wink at the hand. Yet let that be,
> Which the eye fears when it is done to see.　　*(lines 50–3)*

This short scene does little to develop the play's narrative. Instead, it anticipates events that follow, and it has a striking effect in creating the social context, especially the relationship of king and subjects. Whether played as sincere and honest or politically devious, Duncan uses language to claim for himself an ideal form of leadership. After the past of war and treachery, he foresees a prosperous future for Scotland, which depends on the naturalness of social duties and rewards: he will 'plant' and then preside over 'growing'. Banquo picks up the image by promising a 'harvest'. The king's joy is uninhibited in that he laughs at its fullness leading to tears, and as he leaves he invents the idea of being fed by hearing praises of Macbeth. He even manages a comically gracious pun on 'Banquo'/'banquet' so that both generals are included in the celebration.

Act 1 Scene 5

Lady Macbeth is reading the letter that her husband has written about meeting the Witches. Instinctively, she prepares to convince him by speaking to his imaginary presence. She feels that her husband possesses high public achievement: 'Glamis thou art, and Cawdor'. His future will be even more impressive: 'and shalt be / What thou art promised'. She does not mention 'king', perhaps superstitiously, like Macbeth in Scene 3, because naming the great prize might bring bad luck. But she sneers at what she considers his weakness: 'th'milk of human kindness'. She feels she must find 'valour' in her tongue to persuade Macbeth to abandon those scruples which prevent him from seizing the crown. She will have to supply the passion that can motivate him.

A messenger brings news that 'The king comes here tonight.' Macbeth had been granted Cawdor only moments after the Witches had prophesied the honour. Now his wife is granted Duncan in their home just as she is preparing herself to persuade Macbeth to accept murder as the only route to the crown:

> The raven himself is hoarse,
> That croaks the fatal entrance of Duncan
> Under my battlements.   *(lines 36–8)*

The news is unexpected and it provokes her into envisaging a great destiny for herself and her husband. Her special role in achieving this destiny is implied in 'my battlements' ('my' is often stressed in performance) and in the powerful lines that follow.

She calls for 'spirits' more powerful than her own. To retain womanly feelings would inhibit both action and her persuasive powers, and so she orders the spirits to 'unsex' her. There is great erotic force in her urgency to renounce her sex and to replace compassion with 'direst cruelty'. The speech is intense in its imperatives: 'Come, you spirits . . .'; 'Come to my woman's breasts . . .'; 'Come, thick night . . .'. She is prepared for 'murd'ring ministers' to poison her breast milk so that when the blackest night does arrive, she will have the resolve to use the 'keen knife' herself. The final image of heaven peeping suggests that goodness itself is too frail to challenge the world of darkness and horror she is invoking.

In some productions Macbeth arrives to interrupt her vision, even to be a fascinated audience for her last lines. Her ceremonial threefold greeting echoes that of the Witches in Scene 3:

> Great Glamis, worthy Cawdor,
> Greater than both by the all-hail hereafter   *(lines 52–3)*

In performance their first meeting acquires far more significance than its brevity on the page suggests. His words of affection are simply 'My dearest love'. This is enough for most actors to demonstrate the sexual chemistry between them. She aims to seduce him by celebrating his manhood, even though in her earlier soliloquy she makes it clear she doubts his resolve. She does not use the word 'king' and neither of them mentions 'murder', but they understand each other well. She hides her murderous intentions in euphemisms: 'the all-hail hereafter'; 'O never / Shall sun that morrow see'; 'He that's coming / Must be provided for'; 'This night's great business'.

Shakespeare has delayed this first meeting of the two central characters. It lasts for a mere 20 lines and Lady Macbeth entirely dominates it. As Macbeth was 'rapt' in Scene 3, here too he seems lost for words, but she feels his silence is far too eloquent: people looking at his face 'May read strange matters'. She instructs him in the arts of hypocrisy, while she herself takes on the role of managing events:

> look like th'innocent flower,
> But be the serpent under't. He that's coming
> Must be provided for, and you shall put
> This night's great business into my dispatch   *(lines 63–7)*

Act 1 Scene 6

This short scene shows Duncan arriving at the castle and greeting his hostess. Macbeth is absent, though the scene has been played with him lurking unnoticed by the arriving guests and watching Lady Macbeth demonstrate the false courtesies she had declared in Scene 5 to be necessary.

The scene is rich in irony. Duncan seems to forget he has recently been deceived by appearances as he declares the castle to have an aura that guarantees peace and calm. Banquo continues this theme of deception by drawing imagery from nature: the martlets, birds considered by the Jacobeans to be easily deceived, have turned battlements into nesting places:

> Where they most breed and haunt, I have observed
> The air is delicate.   *(lines 9–10)*

Duncan is skilful in paying tribute to individuals. He seems always courteous and sometimes laces his speech with affectionate humour, as, for example, when he tries out Macbeth's new title: 'Where's the Thane of Cawdor?', not 'Glamis' or 'Macbeth' or 'our host'. In the 1976 RSC production, which gave a notably benign view of Duncan, the king invited laughter from the other guests with his self-conscious version of this title, and continued the performance of pedantry with the hunting metaphor which follows. Such laughter, when affectionate, deepens the sense (for an audience) that all the guests are off their guard, particularly as Duncan refers to Macbeth's 'great love', which he describes with unwitting irony as 'sharp as his spur'.

The courtesies continue. Duncan asks to be led into the castle and his final words are 'By your leave, hostess.' Most productions take this to mean that he asks permission to kiss Lady Macbeth. With this final sign of gentleness and trust, he leaves the stage – and will never be seen again.

Act 1 Scene 7

Inside the castle, Duncan is being welcomed with a banquet. Feasting and the formal procedures that go with it are traditionally intended to assert the values of a community at ease with itself. However, Shakespeare chooses not to show the community together. The audience may imagine them offstage but without their host. Macbeth, who should be ministering to his king and other guests, has left them to wrestle with his private tensions.

The audience hears Macbeth's struggle in the soliloquy which opens the scene. He begins by wishing for the impossible. He would want quick action if that could also prevent all consequences, but he recognises the truth that human actions never exist in isolation. They 'return / To plague th'inventor'. This first section of the speech ends with the potent image of a 'poisoned chalice'. There are connotations of the Catholic mass in the offer of a chalice: to poison it would be a horrifying desecration. Macbeth's thoughts move to his relationship with Duncan and the king's special qualities. The arguments against murdering such a guest, kinsman and king are overwhelming. There can be no evading this truth and the verse builds into a cosmic image of horror and protest:

> his virtues
> Will plead like angels, trumpet-tongued against
> The deep damnation of his taking-off.
> And pity, like a naked newborn babe
> Striding the blast, or heaven's cherubin horsed
> Upon the sightless couriers of the air,
> Shall blow the horrid deed in every eye,
> That tears shall drown the wind.   *(lines 18–25)*

Pity, personified in the image of the 'newborn babe', is here supported by the militant power of heavenly goodness. The image makes a striking contrast with Lady Macbeth's view in Scene 5 of heaven peeping impotently 'through the blanket of the dark'. Pity is often thought to be a quiet and private virtue, but Macbeth's imagination merges the picture of an eye watering from the force of a gale with universal weeping and a great public protest against the worst of crimes.

The soliloquy ends with Macbeth personified as ambition, who vaults onto his horse, but, overreaching himself in the leap, collapses on the other side. He has suddenly switched from cosmic protest to the absurdity of the horseman who has misjudged his aim.

Macbeth now seems resolved. He tells his wife, 'We will proceed no further in this business.' She, tense from his absence, has come to remonstrate and realises that she has to begin her urging all over again. What follows is one of the greatest persuasion scenes in all drama. Her aggression and scorn are overwhelming. She uses stabbing rhetorical questions and is quick with repartee when speaking of 'coward', 'man' and 'beast'. She seals up the persuasion with a horrifyingly inhuman image of a woman who dashes out the brains of her suckling child. Some actors construct a past for their marriage that includes a lost child, a subject that is too painful to speak of. At this moment Lady Macbeth may break the taboo in order to persuade Macbeth that he too should abandon a similar prohibition: killing the king.

It was once commonplace for critics to use this powerful image to speculate about the Macbeth family: L C Knights mocked their speculations in his famous essay 'How Many Children Had Lady Macbeth?' But Lady Macbeth's real point lies in its context: she says she would do what all women would find totally abhorrent in order to shame Macbeth into keeping his word to her.

Lady Macbeth sweeps aside her husband's question about failure. She organises the detailed procedures for murdering Duncan, which include drugging the two chamberlains and accusing them of the crime. She reminds Macbeth to give a convincing performance of 'griefs and clamour'. Her persuasion succeeds and his last line shows that he is resolved to follow her instruction and accept the need for hypocrisy:

False face must hide what the false heart doth know.   *(line 82)*

However, Macbeth still regards the murder as 'this terrible feat'. Even though she has persuaded him to kill the king, events will show that he cannot escape the vision of moral and imaginative consequences that he expressed in his soliloquy at the start of the scene.

Act 1: Critical review

Act 1 is violent and hectic. Military events are described in extreme language and all news is brought in a rush. There is little time for reflection as most characters react immediately to what they hear. Only Macbeth and Lady Macbeth reveal their inner thoughts.

The political world of the play seems fragile. The threats of invasion and civil war are only just removed before Macbeth, urged strongly by his wife, plans to murder the king. Shakespeare also presents another threat: the supernatural world of the Witches and their apparent contact with powerful, malevolent forces. The atmosphere of Act 1 is dark and dangerous. Much of the action takes place at night.

Most of the scenes are short, and Shakespeare juxtaposes different locations and groups of characters. In Scenes 1 and 2 the action moves from Witches to king and does so again in Scenes 3 and 4. This pendulum-like method of dramatic construction adds to the sense of antithesis that expresses much of the play's meaning. There is one peaceful moment: Scene 6, where King Duncan fatally misjudges the tranquil appearance of Macbeth's castle. The king seems vulnerable partly because the scene comes between Lady Macbeth's plans for the murder and Macbeth's soliloquy about its horror.

At first the leading characters remain in the background. Macbeth's entry is delayed; his wife does not appear until Scene 5. In his first scene Duncan does little more than receive messages and express gratitude. It is the Witches and the two hasty bringers of news, the Captain and Ross, who create dramatic impact in early scenes.

As with many of his tragic figures, Shakespeare makes a telling distinction between the public hero and the private man. Act 1 celebrates Macbeth as a military leader, but the subtler dramatic value is in his struggle to deal with the temptations that high public honours will place on his integrity and personal honour. His soliloquies show him struggling with something frighteningly unfamiliar.

Act 1 ends with a strong sense of anticipation. The murder is planned but not yet committed. Macbeth and his wife have very different attitudes to their enterprise: it is not yet clear whether 'the deed' will bring them closer or drive them apart.

Act 2 Scene 1

Duncan has been established as potential victim, but Shakespeare now introduces a new type of innocence in Fleance, Banquo's young son. Most productions will have already portrayed the intimacy of father and son by making Fleance a silent part of Duncan's arrival group in Act 1 Scene 6.

This scene takes place out of doors. Perhaps the feast felt oppressive and Banquo has come out for a breath of air before going to bed. Fleance carries a torch; his father looks to the stars for assurance but there is no light to be seen. Banquo tries to joke his way out of unease: 'There's husbandry in heaven'. There is poignancy in the worried father questioning his son, handing over his sword and trying to pray, but the words of the prayer are evasive: he speaks of having 'cursèd thoughts'.

Macbeth is also still up, presumably waiting for a quiet time to murder the king; Banquo is surprised to see him and the two generals engage in uneasy pleasantries. Banquo is more fluent and gives to his host Duncan's present of a diamond for Lady Macbeth (perhaps it is the unspecified 'that' which he gave to Fleance in line 5?). Macbeth needs security as much as Banquo does, and so he moves obliquely towards what seems like a bribe for the other's support. Banquo appears not to recognise the offer (or perhaps he pretends ignorance) and ends the dialogue about 'honour' with a firm statement about genuine integrity. They part, each man increasingly suspicious of the other.

Macbeth gives his servant an instruction about 'my drink' that seems like a coded pre-arrangement with his wife. The 1976 RSC production gave extra tension to this moment by having Macbeth unaware of the servant's presence: he felt the man's hands on his shoulders, putting on a cloak. The shock added intensity to the mental pressure that gives rise to the next soliloquy, Macbeth's hallucination of the dagger. The imaginary dagger is both a warning and an invitation. It is a 'fatal' vision and it has 'gouts of blood', but it also leads him on. At first, Macbeth is terrified and tries to argue away the dagger's existence:

> Art thou not, fatal vision, sensible
> To feeling as to sight? Or art thou but
> A dagger of the mind, a false creation,
> Proceeding from the heat-oppressèd brain?   *(lines 36–9)*

He is questioning the reliability of his senses – can he trust sight more than touch? His senses are not working in harmony as they should. Halfway through the soliloquy he changes his approach: rather than resist the horror, he will intensify it and he begins what seems almost a chant with the words 'Now o'er the one half-world . . .'. He imagines a personified 'Witchcraft', more powerful than witches, celebrating the sacrifices of Hecate, the goddess of sorcery. In comparing himself to Prince Tarquin, who raped Lucretia, Macbeth gives a sinister sexual excitement to his furtive murder of Duncan. He now requires horror as a necessary condition for mental survival. Only by fully entering this new world of evil can he find an alternative 'security'.

At the end of the scene a bell rings, a sudden sound effect that is both alarming and, in Macbeth's mind, an accomplice: 'The bell invites me.' Many productions play this as the thin, slight sound of a handbell to contrast with the deeper significance which Macbeth knows it to have:

> Hear it not, Duncan, for it is a knell
> That summons thee to heaven or to hell.　　　　　*(lines 63–4)*

Act 2 Scene 2

As Macbeth exits at the end of Scene 1, his wife enters immediately. The sleeping king will be murdered offstage. This may seem strange in a play that speaks so directly about bloodshed, but Shakespeare is reinforcing the several taboos about this particular murder: Duncan is Macbeth's guest, cousin and king. The horror of the act will be less about the physical blood and more about the moral significance of the murder, which contributes to all the panicky misunderstandings between Macbeth and his wife in this scene. She has prepared the daggers for him to commit the deed and she has drugged Duncan's grooms into a stupor, but she has needed alcohol to suppress her nerves.

Macbeth enters carrying the bloodstained daggers. The audience sees these immediately, but such is the intensity that Lady Macbeth does not notice them for about 25 lines and he appears unaware that they are still in his hands. He concentrates on the circumstances of the bedchamber; significantly, he never describes the deed itself: another evasion. The grooms prayed in their sleep, but Macbeth, who wanted to join with an 'Amen', was excluded; the word stuck in his throat. He becomes obsessed by the thwarted prayer and by the notion of sleep, which he has now destroyed for ever:

> Methought I heard a voice cry, 'Sleep no more:
> Macbeth does murder sleep', the innocent sleep,
> Sleep that knits up the ravelled sleeve of care,
> The death of each day's life, sore labour's bath,
> Balm of hurt minds, great nature's second course,
> Chief nourisher in life's feast.   *(lines 38–43)*

Macbeth's self-condemnation is reinforced by his memory of the unspecified voice crying out in protest, repeating the word 'sleep' and listing the epithets that speak of calm, healing and nourishment. By destroying what is positive in nature, Macbeth has become 'a man forbid', or accursed, as the Witches prophesied for his sailor-double in Act I Scene 3.

Macbeth's obsessed speech, bursting out after long-suppressed tension, seems unstoppable, until at last Lady Macbeth makes him listen to her. She is appalled by his naivety in bringing the daggers with him and she urges him to gain composure by concentrating on practical matters. He refuses to return and leave the daggers beside the sleeping grooms, on whom they will pin the blame. It is typical of the difference between them that she plans to avoid blame, while he thinks more imaginatively of the wider meaning of their deed. She exits with a grotesque pun:

> If he do bleed,
> I'll gild the faces of the grooms withal,
> For it must seem their guilt.   *(lines 58–60)*

Apart from the lines' obvious meaning of painting their faces with the king's blood, she may be implying that an active conscience that can feel 'guilt' is merely a decorative extra to a human being; it misleads by adding surface 'gilt'. Shakespeare may also be referring to a Jacobean superstition that a murdered man bleeds afresh in the presence of his murderer.

Macbeth is left alone, fascinated by his bloodstained hands. For him the significance of his deed has spread to the whole world: 'all great Neptune's ocean' would not be able to cleanse him. In powerful contrast, when Lady Macbeth joins him, she also displays bloodstained hands, but for her the blood is easily washed away.

They hear a knocking at the castle gate. Macbeth, the former man of action, remains locked within his imagination, thinking (as his wife had put it) 'So brain-sickly of things'. She takes the lead again: they must quickly wash and dress. In one production husband and wife helped each other out of the room, trying to avoid staining their clothes with the blood; the visual effect was that they combined to form an inhuman single creature moving awkwardly towards the door. As the knocking continues, Macbeth's final words express his dismay:

Wake Duncan with thy knocking: I would thou couldst.

(line 77)

Act 2 Scene 3

The sound of knocking links the two scenes. Beginning at line 60 in Scene 2, it continues for another 17 lines, and it brings onstage a new character. The Porter and his comic, bawdy language have sometimes been considered inappropriate. Some eighteenth- and nineteenth-century productions omitted him altogether. However, most modern productions value a short period of relief from the intensity of the last two scenes and recognise that the main dramatic function is to connect the comic Porter thematically with the serious action. For example, he is drunk and thinks he is 'porter of hell-gate' (see page 65). Macbeth also suffers mental confusion; in murdering the king he has done the devil's work and now, in effect, presides over the castle of hell.

'Equivocation' is an important motif in the Porter's imaginative ramblings. The word, meaning to speak with deliberate ambiguity, acquired shifty connotations in the early 1600s when the Jesuit Henry Garnet was accused of involvement in the gunpowder plot. Garnet argued that he had the right to equivocate in self-defence: to mislead his interrogators without actually lying. Hence the Porter's comment on 'an equivocator that could swear in both the scales against either scale'. Such cunning might keep Garnet secure on earth, yet he 'could not equivocate to heaven'. Similarly, Lady Macbeth has urged her husband into skilful deceit, but, unlike her, he has understood that his moral predicament is inescapable.

The knocking on the gate continues, and eventually the Porter admits Macduff and Lennox and jokes about drink (see page 87). Macduff leaves to call on the king, while Macbeth waits for the horrified discovery. He is too preoccupied to find many words to make conversation with Lennox, who describes a terrifying night just gone by:

> The night has been unruly: where we lay,
> Our chimneys were blown down, and, as they say,
> Lamentings heard i'th'air, strange screams of death
>
> *(lines 46–8)*

In *King Lear* and *Julius Caesar* Shakespeare also intensifies similar moments of special disaster on earth with comparable disorder in nature and the heavens. Contemporary belief saw close connections between the social, political, natural and cosmic worlds.

Lennox speaks in wonder of unprecedented horror and refers to reports that the whole earth is diseased. Macbeth clearly understands the significance of what he hears, but in the strain of waiting he manages just the laconic line: ''Twas a rough night.' In performance, this can raise audience laughter, a sign of tension relaxed for a moment before the next period of pressure, which begins with Macduff's entry. He is so horrified that again language seems inadequate to mark or describe the event:

> Tongue nor heart cannot conceive, nor name thee.   *(line 57)*

Macduff is forced into extreme paradox and hyperbole: 'Confusion' becomes a perverse creator or artist producing a 'masterpiece'; Duncan is 'The Lord's anointed temple'; the chamber contains a 'Gorgon' that will destroy sight; the sleepers will arise, as at the final Judgement Day, to witness 'The great doom's image'. He calls for the bell to ring, and this time it will be the 'knell' that Macbeth had predicted. Many productions end this section of the play's series of sound effects with a deeply resonant tolling.

The sound wakes and brings everyone onstage. All feel and express horror, with Macbeth and his wife attempting convincing performances of it. Macduff, showing respect for a woman's delicacy, tries to protect Lady Macbeth but his words have unintended irony:

> The repetition in a woman's ear
> Would murder as it fell. *(lines 78–9)*

Macbeth seems impressively eloquent. Some actors convey a sense of careful preparation in his first speech ('Had I but died . . .') and then in his immediate 'care' for Duncan's young sons. Other actors have felt that, since he was regretting the murder before he committed it, he genuinely feels that 'from this instant, / There's nothing serious in mortality' and that 'The wine of life is drawn'. In contrast, Lady Macbeth is virtually silent after her short opening question. Most actors play her watching Macbeth carefully, worried about his ability to perform his distress.

Macbeth reveals that he has killed Duncan's guards and pretends to regret his impulsiveness. He implies that he had snatched the brief time while the bell was tolling to inspect the chamber by himself and that he had slain the guards without thought or investigation. His sole motive, he says, was love for the king and horror at what had happened to him and he appears to challenge his onstage audience:

> Who could refrain,
> That had a heart to love and in that heart
> Courage to make's love known? *(lines 109–11)*

One actor directed these lines at Lady Macbeth to convey the private meaning that he killed both the grooms and Duncan to prove to her his courageous manhood and to make himself worthy of her love. Lady Macbeth's response is 'Help me hence, ho', and in many productions she faints. Critics and actors interpret this moment in different ways. Perhaps she feels that Macbeth's murder of the grooms and subsequent explanation are so dangerous that she needs to buy time, and so contrives the faint to distract the others. Perhaps she is genuinely overwhelmed by shock or perhaps she is recognising the beginnings of his new independence that may break the bonds between them.

Shakespeare also focuses on the bewildered shock of others, most vividly seen in Malcolm and Donaldbain. While Banquo, as senior general-turned-statesman, takes charge and asserts integrity ('In the great hand of God I stand'), Duncan's sons find two brief moments to plan their future. They recognise both their appalling danger and their obligation to take a lead in this crisis. The only solution is escape since, looking round at all the horrified faces, it is impossible for them to distinguish the true man from the murderous hypocrite: there are indeed 'daggers in men's smiles'. Malcolm plans to head for England and Donaldbain for Ireland and the scene ends with a succinct and punning couplet:

> There's warrant in that theft
> Which steals itself when there's no mercy left.   *(lines 138–9)*

There are two puns: 'warrant' meaning that the action is justified and also a document used to arrest a thief; 'steal' meaning the action of a thief and also describing furtive movement. The effect of the couplet is to suggest that now, in a new era in which there is 'no mercy left', it will be necessary even for good men to employ shifty manoeuvres. Malcolm will not reappear until Act 4. By then the audience will learn whether his 'tears' have 'brewed', his grief matured into policy and action.

Act 2 Scene 4

This scene slows the onstage action with a type of choric commentary, yet hurries the offstage story of Macbeth's route to the crown. An old man discusses the significance of recent events with Ross. Their descriptions echo Lennox's speech in the previous scene, in which he spoke of disasters in nature matching the horrors on earth. The heavens, like an audience, are appalled by the actions of men on their earthly stage. The basic distinctions of day and night, light and darkness are confused, so acting as a comment on the whole of Act 2. The first two scenes took place in darkness, and before the sun rose for the third scene, Duncan and his values were destroyed. The state of nature now ensures that

> darkness does the face of earth entomb
> When living light should kiss it   *(lines 9–10)*

The two men speak of reversals in nature which express their feeling about the destroyed relationship of subject to king: an owl has killed a hawk, and it is said that Duncan's horses ate each other.

Macduff gives information about offstage events. The official view is that the grooms murdered the king, paid to do it by Malcolm and Donaldbain, who have now fled the country. Macbeth has been named as king and has gone to Scone for his coronation. Duncan's body is to be buried beside the bones of the dead kings of Scotland. Macduff conveys all this information in a few lines without comment. However, he is introduced as 'the good Macduff' and Shakespeare's audiences, who responded to his role in Scene 2 as echoing *The Harrowing of Hell* (see page 65), will expect him to challenge Macbeth. In most productions he speaks with angry ironic brevity: his attitude shows him as clearly hostile to Macbeth, but on the surface his words follow the official line on events. His wariness is not that of a criminal, but of a man intending to mount a campaign against Macbeth and uncertain as to who is friend and who foe.

Macduff dangerously decides to stay away from Macbeth's ceremonies and plans to return to his home in Fife. He ends by speaking sceptically of the new regime:

> Well may you see things well done there. Adieu,
> Lest our old robes sit easier than our new.   *(lines 37–8)*

On the surface he refers to coronation robes, but his comment fits with the imagery of clothes as attitudes; life under the new rule of Macbeth is likely to prove difficult.

The Old Man watches silently through the second half of this scene, but ends it with a couplet recommending good men to make the best of bad circumstances. His dramatic function has been to represent wisdom and long experience, which react against the horrific nature of this murder. His final couplet may be taken as the words of a wise man taking the very long view to a time beyond the reign of Macbeth. However, in performance, it may have a trite effect, suggesting that traditional wisdom is helpless in these uniquely dreadful times.

> God's benison go with you, and with those
> That would make good of bad, and friends of foes.
>
> *(lines 40–1)*

Act 2: Critical review

Act 2 contains the crucial event of Duncan's murder, unusually early for the great turning point of a tragedy. It happens offstage, and the onstage action shows the characters' responses to it. Almost all express horror, even Macbeth himself, who knows that violent actions 'return / To plague th'inventor'.

Shakespeare varies the narrative pace. Scene 1 is tense with waiting, and focuses on Macbeth's mental strain, especially in the dagger soliloquy. Scene 2 accelerates into the hectic anxiety of husband and wife. The action then pauses with the Porter, whose comedy relaxes the tension but comments on the main themes and is made threatening by the continuous sound of knocking at the gate. In the act so far no more than three characters have been onstage at once, but the offstage discovery of the murder brings on other characters and a burst of new energy. The focus moves potently to record the various reactions of Banquo, Macduff, Malcolm, Macbeth, Lady Macbeth. The act ends with a pause in the narrative, as Ross and the Old Man comment on the significance of the disaster.

Much of the act's imagery concentrates on the disruption in nature. Sleep is the nourishing gift of nature, and when Macbeth speaks of a personified 'sleep' which he has murdered, he indicates the irreparable damage he has done also within himself. Duncan's murder provokes images of grotesque and violent effects in the cosmic and animal worlds.

Macbeth again appears to rescue Scotland from a great crisis. In Act 1 Duncan applauded his great military success for the public good. Now Duncan's death means a strong leader is required and Macbeth's experience and distinction seem to be necessary qualifications. But Act 2 raises questions which Act 3 will address:

- Will Banquo's suspicions of Macbeth deepen?
- Will Macduff's opposition become more overt?
- Can Macbeth suppress his tormented thoughts?
- How will the relationship of husband and wife develop when they are king and queen?
- Will Macbeth's regime be different from Duncan's?

Act 3 Scene 1

Act 2 ended with the implication that Macduff would challenge Macbeth. Act 3 begins with Macbeth's other potential opponent. Banquo is the only person to have seen Macbeth with the Witches, and their prophecies also included him. He responded evasively to Macbeth's overtures, but he also stated publicly that he will fight against 'treasonous malice'.

Macbeth is now king, but though Banquo fears that he achieved his aim 'most foully', his soliloquy does not develop this unease into clear opposition. Instead, his thoughts turn to the prospects of his descendants. Some critics believe that the play is intended partly as a tribute to King James I and the Stuart family, which claimed to spring from Banquo and Fleance (see page 75). However, Banquo's soliloquy seems to compromise his honour: he is beginning to think deviously.

Macbeth enters and pays special regard to Banquo. This is his first appearance as king, and some productions show his new status by giving him a crown and sceptre. Some have even included a coronation in dumbshow at the beginning of the scene, with Banquo uneasy at the ceremony and absenting himself for private thoughts.

Macbeth gathers detailed information about Banquo's plans for the day and feigns slight disappointment that these prevent Banquo attending a council meeting. He pretends to be generous and flexible: Banquo can advise tomorrow. The stage directions give no indication that Fleance is present, but most productions include him with his father to remind the audience that he must be part of Macbeth's murderous plans, since he is the heir who can ensure that Banquo will be the 'father / Of many kings'.

Macbeth gives the impression that he is an efficient leader: he has up-to-date intelligence about Duncan's 'bloody' sons; he has planned an immediate council meeting. He has ordered a feast; as new king he will welcome and thank his subjects. The public nature of the scene so far requires that Macbeth's behaviour is evidently a conscious performance. What follows will be far more private. He urges everyone to relax and enjoy private time until the evening. He will do likewise:

> we will keep ourself
> Till supper-time alone.   *(lines 44–5)*

In one production, Lady Macbeth felt it natural that she would stay with her husband, but was then suddenly shocked by his word 'alone', which he directed firmly at her. The moment was a strong sign that their partnership was breaking. Though they were king and queen, the evil they had committed was beginning to drive them into their separate worlds.

Macbeth tells a servant to bring in 'those men' and alone onstage describes his feelings about what he hoped would be his crowning achievement: 'To be thus is nothing'. This soliloquy is dispirited. He broods on Banquo's presence inhibiting his power to think or act. Thinking about Banquo's integrity, he praises his mixture of 'dauntless temper' and political prudence:

> He hath a wisdom that doth guide his valour
> To act in safety.   *(lines 54–5)*

Macbeth analyses his own achievement and finds it to be 'fruitless' and 'barren'. He is angry that he seems to have damaged his soul ('mine eternal jewel') simply to hand over all the benefits to 'Banquo's issue': the descendants who will rule in Scotland. For much of Acts 1 and 2 Macbeth seemed introspective, as Lady Macbeth several times complained, but now he decides on an energetic challenge against his fate. In this mood he is ready to instruct the two men who arrive.

They are ruined, desperate men, eager for employment and unscrupulous about how they earn their money. Macbeth is starting his reign not by working through his noblemen, but by operating furtively, like a grubby dictator using low-status, resentful outcasts. He is employing them to murder Banquo and he handles them with ruthless efficiency. He refers to a previous meeting, touching vaguely on 'evidence' that he had contrived for them. He sneers, in the word 'gospelled', at any notion of Christian patience or forgiveness that real 'men' might possess. His sneer recalls his exchange with Lady Macbeth in Act 1 Scene 7, when she taunted him about the nature of true manliness. Here he uses a similar argument, developing it into a comparison between men and dogs. For a modern audience this may feel like a curious pause in his persuasion, but Jacobeans would recognise the comparison as an example of appropriate rhetorical technique:

> Ay, in the catalogue ye go for men,
> As hounds, and greyhounds, mongrels, spaniels, curs,
> Shoughs, water-rugs, and demi-wolves are clept
> All by the name of dogs.   *(lines 91–4)*

There are distinctions between men, as with dogs, and Macbeth urges the murderers to be like 'The valued file': the best types. The effect of Macbeth's list is to set up a new system of values for a new reign, suggesting that dog-like qualities will now replace what in Duncan's regime was 'The valued file' in humanity: the noblest virtues. Fine distinctions between types of loyalty, honour, goodness, etc. now seem perverted in the catalogue of dogs.

When the men confess that life has treated them badly, Macbeth plays the role of confiding to them that he is trapped by Banquo's presence. He argues that he needs to appear above reproach so as to keep on side the 'certain friends that are both his and mine'. Shakespeare shows the breakdown of integrity in the new regime: the king uses the argument that hypocrisy is necessary in political life as a technique of government.

Macbeth gives a rapid list of instructions about the practical business of the murder. Fleance too must die, though Macbeth gives no clear reason. The murderers express no qualms about killing a child. Macbeth ends the meeting abruptly. His crisp final couplet seems to express satisfaction with the first political act of his reign. There is confidence in his jeer that Banquo is going on a new journey, to his death:

> It is concluded. Banquo, thy soul's flight,
> If it find heaven, must find it out tonight.   *(lines 140–1)*

Act 3 Scene 2

After the ceremony and plotting of Scene 1, this is a private, more domestic scene. From the beginning Shakespeare stresses Lady Macbeth's isolation. She questions a servant for information, then formally requests an audience with 'the king'. She echoes the sense of loss expressed in Macbeth's previous soliloquy:

> Nought's had, all's spent
> Where our desire is got without content.

'Tis safer to be that which we destroy
Than by destruction dwell in doubtful joy.   *(lines 4–7)*

'All's spent' conveys great weariness and 'got' is a blunt, flat word to
describe their achievement. The heavy rhythms of the antitheses in
her two rhyming couplets suggest that she lacks the reserves of energy
that she needs to reach out towards her husband's troubled spirit. Her
reproachful words when she greets him have lost the persuasive
power of her language in Act I. Macbeth continues to brood on the
danger both from his enemies and also from the debilitating horror
that lies within his imagination. He speaks of 'terrible dreams' and
'torture' and 'restless ecstasy'. The word 'ecstasy' describes an extreme
emotional state, whether of delight or torment. It suggests that there
is no control or balance about his mind. He lives *ex stasis* or outside a
state of control.

Macbeth feels Duncan has gained the benefit: 'he sleeps well'. But
the words suggest that the 'fitful fever', which Duncan has escaped,
describes Macbeth's life far more accurately. It is darkly ironic that his
opponents (murdered or soon to be murdered) are the beneficiaries,
whilst the murderer is living a nightmare. Fate is making a joke of
Macbeth's expectations: the criminal is becoming victim, tortured by
terrible dreams.

But Macbeth remains defiant, and when at last he responds to his
wife, he plays a curious trick on her: he urges her to pay especially
courteous attention to Banquo at the feast in the evening. He deplores
the fact that their safety depends on careful concealment, and
agonises that his mind is 'full of scorpions' whilst Banquo and
Fleance live. He tells her nothing of his instructions to the Murderers,
but only that 'there shall be done / A deed of dreadful note.'

A great change has come over their relationship. She speaks very
little in the second half of the scene, while Macbeth evokes terrifying
and intense images:

Light thickens,
And the crow makes wing to th'rooky wood;
Good things of day begin to droop and drowse,
Whiles night's black agents to their preys do rouse.

(lines 50–3)

The intensity of Macbeth's language recalls his 'dagger' soliloquy just before the murder and also Lady Macbeth's invocation before his arrival in Act 1 Scene 5. To survive mentally and to find the strength to continue, they have to imagine a new world of evil, and almost conjure it into existence: 'Come, seeling night . . .'. Macbeth seems like a magician or alchemist performing his mysteries.

Act 3 Scene 3

The two Murderers prepare for action, but a mysterious third figure has joined them. Many productions use this unnamed character in various scenes in the play's second half to suggest that Macbeth is never sure of his chosen subordinates and always needs to set spies on them. It has even been suggested that the Third Murderer could be Macbeth himself, but that interpretation poses practical problems because of his behaviour in the next scene.

The Murderers are apprehensive and disagree, but their talk is of gentler aspects of everyday life, with the sun going down and late travellers reaching their resting places. It is normal for people approaching the palace to leave their horses and cover the final stretch on foot. Such moments of ordinary life contrast with and so heighten the violation about to be committed.

Banquo appears, has no time to defend himself and is struck down. Somehow the light he carries is extinguished and Fleance escapes under the cover of darkness. The Third Murderer rebukes his bungling companions; all of them know that Fleance had to be killed too.

Act 3 Scene 4

This scene dramatises a feast, the first formal and community occasion of Macbeth's reign. In this traditional and warlike culture a feast expresses the harmony between king and subject. It embodies the hierarchy (within the nobility) that gives guests the security of knowing their positions. Macbeth has violated all this, and so his behaviour as host is merely an elaborate pretence, filling the scene with irony. Macbeth's first lines refer to this social hierarchy: 'You know your own degrees'. He promises to 'play the humble host', seemingly unaware of the irony in the word 'play'. The king, as host, promises to humble himself for the evening by attending to the needs of his guests. The wider sense of 'play' suggests to the audience that all his behaviour is as insincere as his position of king is false.

Lady Macbeth 'keeps her state', which may be interpreted as her sitting apart on the throne. The Old Vic production in 1973 dressed her in jewel-encrusted robes for this important occasion, but with her drained spirit, so evident in Act 3 Scene 2, she looked like a painted doll. The clothes seemed to mock the wearer.

The First Murderer enters quietly, and the dramatic focus leaves the feasting to show Macbeth's reactions as the Murderer tells what has happened. Macbeth is alarmed to see blood on the Murderer's face. A previous bloodstained messenger appeared in Act 1 when the Captain reported to Duncan. Then the blood was a hero's mark of distinction: here in the banquet hall it must not be detected. Macbeth's relief at hearing of Banquo's death is immediately undercut by the news of Fleance's escape. Describing his mental state, he uses images that convey inhibition: 'cabined, cribbed, confined, bound in'. The play continues to show that the effect of evil deeds occur just as much within the criminal's mind as in the social and political world he is creating.

Lady Macbeth reminds her husband of his obligations as host. She knows nothing of the Murderer's presence. During the Act 1 banquet for Duncan, Macbeth was too disturbed to remain in the room; in this banquet too he will be, in effect, absent from his guests, locked in obsessive introspection. His outward behaviour becomes erratic, swinging between private struggle and a forced jovial hospitality. His words challenge the anxiety he feels: he publicly regrets Banquo's absence and hopes that no 'mischance' has happened to him. Ross asks Macbeth to join them and Lennox points to an empty chair, but Macbeth declares the table full. He sees what the lords cannot: that the blood-streaked ghost of Banquo has joined the company. There is grim comedy in the lines that follow:

> Thou canst not say I did it; never shake
> Thy gory locks at me! *(lines 50–1)*

Strictly speaking, Macbeth is telling the truth: he did not murder Banquo, but this is a desperate piece of equivocation, which will neither deter the ghost nor settle Macbeth's nerves. Directors have a clear choice here. They can present the apparition as a bodily presence, using the actor who plays Banquo, demonstrating what Macbeth sees and so increasing the visual shock of the scene. Or they can offer the audience the view that the noblemen see: Macbeth's inexplicable horror as he looks at what seems to them an empty chair.

Lady Macbeth now has only partial contact with her husband, but struggles to calm him. Crucially for their royal public relations, she must cover up the disaster with invented excuses and reassure the guests. The lords remain silent and the drama focuses on Lady Macbeth trying to shame the king into composure. She tells him that being afraid of ghosts is the stuff of a woman's fireside story and that he is 'unmanned in folly'. Macbeth feverishly explains the terrible paradox he witnesses:

> The time has been
> That when the brains were out, the man would die,
> And there an end. But now they rise again
> With twenty mortal murders on their crowns
> And push us from our stools. *(lines 78–82)*

Shakespeare is prepared to risk dark comedy mixed in with the strain and horror. Macbeth finds no humour himself in the thought of being pushed from his stool by a dead man. Directors and actors have to decide how far to exploit the absurdity of Macbeth's mental plight.

Irony is constantly present. Lady Macbeth lies, claiming that her husband suffers from a childhood illness. Macbeth supports the lie by speaking of his 'strange infirmity', probably without realising that the words also describe the 'strange' sickness of the mind that accompanies his crime. Again he defies his overwrought mind by drinking ostentatiously to Banquo, and again the Ghost appears to him. In defiant rage Macbeth asserts the emptiness of the vision:

> Thy bones are marrowless, thy blood is cold;
> Thou hast no speculation in those eyes
> Which thou dost glare with. *(lines 94–6)*

He is angry at feeling frightened and resents any suggestion of cowardice. He even seems to accuse the Ghost of cowardice for appearing insubstantially. He urges it to appear as a bear, rhinoceros or tiger so that he could fight it as a soldier. When Macbeth speaks of 'Unreal mock'ry', he recognises that he is the victim of some sort of grim joke that the supernatural is playing on him. When the Ghost disappears, he is 'a man again'.

Lady Macbeth can play the gracious hostess no longer and immediately dismisses their guests. Contradicting the opening lines of the scene, she wants no time wasted on social etiquette: they are to go 'At once'. The final 23 lines of dialogue are usually played slowly in a still and eerie atmosphere. The relics of a failed public occasion are evident in the table, chairs, goblets, etc., but the scene is now private. Both seem exhausted. Some productions, suggesting that Lady Macbeth has suffered more than her husband from the horror and shock, have her collapse or faint. In others she removes her crown to signify that her royal ambition is now discredited.

At this point the action of the play pauses, inviting audiences to question how Macbeth's regime can continue and whether husband and wife will suffer together or apart. Some actors believe that Macbeth is perversely liberated into finding new energy now that he has entered the mysterious world of evil that he evoked at the end of Act 3 Scene 2. He broods on 'blood':

It will have blood they say: blood will have blood.

(line 122)

He asks the time, and Lady Macbeth's answer, 'Almost at odds with morning, which is which', catches the play's sense of conflict and blurred perception. Macbeth's mind moves from Banquo to Macduff, his next opponent, who has wanted no part in the royal celebrations. Macbeth has noticed his reluctance: in every nobleman's house he keeps a servant paid to spy and to report back. The new regime is very different from the sense of trust which made Duncan so well loved and so vulnerable.

Macbeth determines to visit the Witches, because knowledge of the future, however bad, may reduce the troubles in his mind. He threatens that there is more blood to be shed. In his imagination, blood is a river; he has waded so far in that it is just as difficult to return as it is to go forward. His powerful image uses antithesis to convey uncertainty. Macbeth could have become paralysed by his fear and exhaustion, but instead he is forcing himself into activity. He intends to reverse the accepted wisdom of good government, whereby careful thought precedes action:

> Strange things I have in head that will to hand,
> Which must be acted ere they may be scanned.

(lines 139–40)

Lady Macbeth can manage no more than a few lines in this final dialogue. Her weariness makes her desperate for sleep. She needs it for herself, and she offers it as the solution for him. Neither of them seems to remember their dialogue in Act 2 Scene 2, when Macbeth knew that he had 'murdered sleep'. He has cut himself off from the essential power of renewal that nature has given to all living creatures. Macbeth ends the scene by seeing himself not as a practised criminal, but as a novice in need of more murderous experience: 'We are yet but young in deed.'

Act 3 Scene 5

This scene (often omitted in modern productions) links the previous scene, in which Macbeth decides to visit the Witches, and the opening of Act 4, in which they prepare for his arrival. Its language is more lyrical than the other supernatural scenes and is commonly thought to have been written by Thomas Middleton (a fellow playwright), either on his own or in collaboration with Shakespeare. The three Witches meet with Hecate, goddess of witchcraft. The role is sometimes played by Lady Macbeth. She rebukes them for not involving her in their plans for Macbeth. He is 'a wayward son', dedicated more to himself than to promoting witchcraft. Hecate refers to his imminent arrival, for which she must perform 'Great business' to raise spirits to mislead him further. She speaks of 'the glory of our art'; this and the song, 'Come away, come away' (which also appears in Middleton's play *The Witch*) suggest that the scene was intended more for theatrical display than for its part in the story of Macbeth. There are opportunities for spectacular stage illusion, such as the flying of Hecate, and masque-like elements of song and dance.

Act 3 Scene 6

Like Act 2 Scene 4, this short scene has a choric function. Lennox and an unnamed Lord consider the rumours that the recent murders have provoked. It appears that all three sons (Malcolm, Donaldbain and Fleance) have been accused of patricide. Macduff failed to attend the state banquet and snubbed Macbeth's messenger. He has fled to

England and has joined Malcolm, who, in self-imposed exile, is being warmly supported by the king, Edward the Confessor.

The scene is similar to Act 2 Scene 4 in another sense. There, Macduff, with heavy irony, feigned support for Macbeth; here, Lennox might appear in his long opening speech to support the outrageous lies and spin that Macbeth continues to spread. Onstage these lines are usually spoken with evident irony. There are moments when Lennox's real feeling appears, particularly when he hopes that Duncan's sons will never find themselves in Macbeth's power: 'under his key'.

This disguise of true feeling usually conveys a feature of Macbeth's regime: that deceit is needed both by those that sustain it and by those who oppose it. In one production a servant of Macbeth passed to and fro during the scene, so compelling Lennox into words that supported the party line. Only when the servant had gone was it possible to speak honestly.

The scene implies that rebellion is gathering but as yet has little effect in Scotland, because Macbeth's tyrannical regime is in control. However, Macduff hopes to establish a crusading force in England. The implication is that this will be a holy war as much as a political one, since King Edward, who welcomes Malcolm, is described as a saint: he is 'pious', he behaves with 'grace', he is a 'holy king' and has the support of God. The Lord recalls the days when Duncan was king and hopes that:

> we may again
> Give to our tables meat, sleep to our nights,
> Free from our feasts and banquets bloody knives,
> Do faithful homage and receive free honours   *(lines 33–6)*

The references to sleep, feasts, honours and faithfulness act as a summary of lost ideals. 'Bloody knives' at banquets describes the violations of community values and recalls the ominous feasts of Act 1 Scene 7 and Act 3 Scene 4. The scene ends with prayers for an end to Scotland's nightmare.

Act 3: Critical review

Act 3 begins with Macbeth as king. He takes immediate steps to establish his new status, proposing a council meeting and a banquet, but planning the murder of Banquo. Banquo is ruthlessly dispatched, but Macbeth's attempts to 'play the humble host' in Scene 4 collapse into an embarrassing shambles and arouse the suspicions of his guests. By the end of Act 3 there are signs of gathering opposition when Lennox and a Lord speak of Macduff's alliance with Malcolm, and a proposed invasion of Scotland.

The act shows Macbeth realising that it is impossible for him to achieve security. Becoming king has not brought an end to his troubles; indeed, he is now acutely aware of threats from below and beyond:

- Malcolm and Donaldbain have escaped, but remain potentially dangerous.
- Banquo has been removed but Fleance has escaped, and so, as 'Banquo's issue', poses a long-term menace.
- Macduff refused to attend both the coronation and the banquet. By the end of Act 3 Macbeth sees him as the most dangerous political enemy.

The appearance of Banquo's ghost shows that Macbeth must face disruptive forces from within his mind as well as from external opponents. The Ghost makes Macbeth realise that he must deal with both types of unrest: political and mental.

The act reveals changes in the relationship between Macbeth and his wife. She had expected the crown to bring security and shared success. But Macbeth is moving into an isolated private world and he pays little attention to her either in the domesticity of Scene 2 or the public arena of Scene 4. She tries to reach and help him, but fails, and by the end of Act 3 she is fatigued and dispirited.

Apart from two brief scenes – Banquo's murder and the scene with Hecate – Act 3 takes place indoors and feels claustrophobic. Macbeth speaks of being 'cabined, cribbed, confined'. The action explores a criminal's tortured mind ('full of scorpions') even more intensely than it portrays the political consequences of killing a king.

Act 4 Scene 1

The Witches are engrossed in an ugly ritual around their cauldron. Their familiars ('the brindled cat', 'the hedge-pig', 'Harpier') have given assent and the time is right for the complicated ceremony. They stir into the boiling mixture fragments of creatures all associated with night-time and black magic. Their 'recipe' includes pieces of reptiles, wolf, shark, goat, tiger, baboon. Human body parts (and signs of the casual racism that was widespread in Shakespeare's time) include 'blaspheming Jew', 'Nose of Turk, and Tartar's lips'. The list becomes more repulsive and the Witches' procedures evoke a sense of danger. King James had ordered death as the punishment for anyone who exhumed bodies for practices of black magic. Hecate appears, approves their work and calls for music, song and dance to celebrate the end of the Witches' preparations. Hecate's speech is often cut in modern productions by directors who feel that the image of 'elves and fairies in a ring' is too tame and more appropriate to an engaging folk tale than to this play's concern with the serious horror of evil.

The Witches sense an intruder approaching, and express their intuition with a strange image of physical sensation:

> By the pricking of my thumbs,
> Something wicked this way comes   *(lines 44–5)*

When Macbeth came upon them in Act 1, the phallic image of 'a pilot's thumb' introduced him. Many productions show that the Witches are eager to welcome Macbeth now through sexual excitement as well as converting him to evil practices. Macbeth urgently demands information. He begins with 'I conjure you . . .', a solemn injunction that they deliver the truth. He follows it with repeated 'Though' clauses, listing disasters in natural and human life. All these he is prepared to tolerate, provided that he has an answer to his questions. His final image is the most awesome:

> though the treasure
> Of nature's germen tumble altogether
> Even till destruction sicken   *(lines 57–9)*

'Nature's germen', or the seeds of all creative life, may be lost for ever, swallowed up by a personified 'destruction' who is sickened by his excess. The consequences of what Macbeth has done, and is still anticipating, are cosmic.

The Witches instantly agree to his demands and indicate that they have 'masters'. Macbeth is moving further towards the centre of their mysteries: the Witches allow him to see more powerful spirits. The 'masters' are either the apparitions which are about to show themselves, or perhaps forces beyond, which manipulate them.

The first apparition is 'an armed Head'. This could represent the military reality that underpins the play, and the violent premise of Macbeth's rule. It may also remind an audience of the play's first reported event, the death of Macdonald, his head severed and placed on battlements. But the apparitions act chiefly as prophets: in this sense the severed head may be foretelling Macbeth's own death as another 'Macdonald'. Macbeth was once a military hero, suppressing rebellion, but he is now about to suffer at the hands of the succeeding hero, as the first apparition warns him to 'beware Macduff'.

The second apparition is 'a bloody Child', who seems to contradict the warning of the first. Macbeth has no need for fear, since he cannot be harmed by anyone born of woman. This apparition has been variously interpreted as:
- Banquo's descendant, smeared with the blood of his murdered ancestor;
- Macduff, prematurely torn from his mother's womb;
- Lady Macbeth dashing out the brains of her child;
- the 'naked newborn babe / Striding the blast', evoked by Macbeth at Act 1 Scene 7, lines 21–2;
- Macduff's children, soon to be slaughtered;
- innocence that is all too vulnerable in Macbeth's Scotland.

Macbeth is reassured by this second apparition, but he determines to 'take a bond of fate', so that the 'promise' cannot be broken. He will continue in his plans to destroy Macduff. He will 'sleep in spite of thunder', and, as if in ironic agreement, Fate seems to reply with a clap of thunder. The sound heralds the third apparition, also a child, but this time he carries a tree in his hand and the threat of blood is replaced by the triumph of a crown.

The child may represent the future, perhaps as Malcolm, the immediate heir to Duncan, or, more distantly, Banquo's children. The tree may indicate growth, both as a family tree and as a sign of nature renewing itself. It challenges Macbeth's readiness to destroy 'nature's germen', and so denies his wishes. But the apparition's speech also reassures Macbeth, who finds hope in the words that he can never be vanquished until Birnam Wood moves towards his castle at Dunsinane. This apparition equivocates in that the visual image of the crowned child disturbs Macbeth, but the words strengthen his hopes.

Macbeth feels immediately threatened by Macduff, but his deeper concern is with Banquo's issue (just as in his soliloquy in Act 3 Scene 1). Shakespeare shows that political and mental stability have become impossible for Macbeth. Moments of optimism are no more than brief glimpses, which serve only to emphasise the reality of bleak despair. The Witches refuse to answer his question about the long-term future; he threatens them with 'an eternal curse' and the cauldron sinks into the ground. With the command 'Show!' thrice repeated, Macbeth is granted a vision, this time without words.

Some directors accept the invitation and show an eerie procession of the eight kings, Banquo and the glass, which shows the future stretching ahead to 'th'crack of doom'. If the play is performed in a smaller, 'studio' setting, then the 'show' (like Banquo's ghost in Act 3) may be a vision that lies only in Macbeth's mind and has no objective stage reality. One production gave added force to his imagination by having the Witches blindfold him before they allowed him to 'see' anything.

The First Witch's lines that follow and are thought to be more of Middleton's additions are sometimes cut. However, the light rhyming couplets can have a helpful ironic value in rounding off the scene of black magic. Before they leave, the Witches perform a dance to cheer his spirits. It may be a parody of a court masque (see page 69), a theatrical tribute that would be expected in Shakespeare's time to entertain the monarch:

> That this great king may kindly say,
> Our duties did his welcome pay.   *(lines 130–1)*

Lennox appears from 'without'. Macbeth is now less guarded in his speech. He asks if Lennox has seen the 'weïrd sisters' and damns those who trust in them. Lennox reports that Macduff has fled to England. Macbeth appears surprised (though the last 20 lines of Act 3

Scene 6 suggested that his own spies have already given information about Macduff). Lennox himself also heard the news. It may be that Shakespeare is inconsistent in plotting his story, but the confusion helps to suggest that Scotland now is rife with rumour, false intelligence, misunderstanding and concealment, and so such discrepancies may not appear as faults of stagecraft, but as helping to establish the unstable political climate.

Macbeth's final speech may be played as a soliloquy. He feels that urgency is the only valid policy. He sees himself as in a battle with time, and feels that purposes are useless without action. He intends that his first thoughts will be translated into immediate action, echoing the view he expressed at the end of Act 3 Scene 4, when he spoke of strange things that 'must be acted ere they may be scanned'. It was a common contention of the time, most notably argued in Thomas Elyot's *The Book of the Governor* (1531), that the ideal ruler combines thought and action in a perfect balance. Too much thought and the king becomes a scholar, remote from political realities; too much action and the country suffers from reckless improvisation.

Macbeth's most brutal thought ends the scene. He plans to attack Macduff's castle and kill all who can be found there. He speaks of those who 'trace him in his line', ignoring the prophecy that it is Banquo's descendants, not Macduff's, who would reign in Scotland. Up until now, Macbeth has always acted against the next immediate threat to his ambition or security: Duncan, then Malcolm, then Banquo, then Macduff. Slaughtering women and children is a reflex action of a man who now kills for the sake of killing.

Act 4 Scene 2

Macbeth's violent impulses are matched by rapid stagecraft that takes the action immediately to Macduff's castle. The dialogue between Lady Macduff and Ross begins in anxious mid-conversation. She is appalled by her husband's flight, seeing it as treachery motivated by fear. Ross's arguments feel unconvincing: he urges her to be patient and to trust in her husband's experience and wisdom. Her reference to the wren being prepared to fight against the owl to defend its young ones recalls the Act 2 images of nature behaving unnaturally in response to Duncan's murder. It seems to Lady Macduff that her husband has succumbed to the destruction of natural impulses; she declares that 'He loves us not.'

Ross seems embarrassed that he is anxious to leave. He no longer argues against her protest, but acknowledges that Macbeth's Scotland is having its effect on the very integrity of all her people:

> But cruel are the times when we are traitors
> And do not know ourselves, when we hold rumour
> From what we fear, yet know not what we fear,
> But float upon a wild and violent sea,
> Each way and none.   *(lines 18–22)*

Ross speaks of human beings fearful and subject to random violence, moving all ways, but in no particular direction. People are uncertain not just about what they perceive, but also about their very identity. Ross seems to be restating Macbeth's perplexity in Act 1 Scene 3, when he struggled with the news of becoming Cawdor just as the Witches had prophesied: 'and nothing is, / But what is not'.

Ross leaves Lady Macduff alone with her son. He is the youngest and least threatening of all the sons of Macbeth's intended victims: Malcolm is safely in England, Fleance escaped, but Macduff's son is simply a vulnerable innocent. His mother tells him that he is, in effect, fatherless. In the play's most intimate and domestic scene their dialogue is both naive and profound, showing both moral confusion and insight. Lady Macduff speaks of adopting an immoral life in buying and selling husbands, as though retaliating against Macduff's treachery to her in leaving Scotland. Their conversation on the nature of treachery ends with the child supplying the pragmatic common sense that liars and swearers are sufficiently strong and numerous to overpower honest men. His words ironically identify what has happened to Scotland. Amongst those honest men who survive, Macduff has fled Scotland and Ross has just left the doomed house.

A messenger warns that danger is very close. He speaks of 'fell cruelty', but he cannot or will not be more specific. As so often in the play, uncertainty makes danger more frightening. The unnamed messenger dares stay no longer than his single speech allows. The tension builds even more strongly towards the family's slaughter. Though glimmers of goodness still exist in Scotland, they are becoming fainter and fainter: men can no longer do anything to protect women, but simply arrive, warn and depart.

Lady Macduff is helpless. She realises that a strong defence of her innocence is pointless in 'this earthly world'. Accepted values are now so changed that people are praised for doing harm and goodness is often 'dangerous folly'. She believes that her husband has become part of this reversal. 'Fair is foul, and foul is fair' aptly describes her disillusion.

The murderers enter, asking for Macduff. Mother and son each make a brief defiance, and the scene ends with Lady Macduff seeing her son killed. Shakespeare spends very few lines on these murders, but the impact in most stage and film performances is horrifying. Some productions show quick, even routine, brutality; in others the murders are committed with lingering pleasure.

Act 4 Scene 3

Malcolm is in England as guest of the saint–king, Edward the Confessor. This is the longest scene of the play, and in many productions it is set in sunlight after so many scenes of darkness. Some designers have used green to signify new growth beginning. Nineteenth-century productions sometimes included foliage and water to create peaceful landscape effects, but some modern directors have continued to stress Malcolm's continuing danger by having uniformed guards protect him.

Malcolm is in mid-dialogue with Macduff. Shakespeare creates a cruelly ironic contrast between Macduff in this peaceful setting and the previous image of his terrified family being struck down. If the play were moving towards a simple moral conclusion of virtuous retribution defeating Macbeth's evil, Macduff and Malcolm would plan together in harmony. However, this does not happen. Shakespeare's moral treatment is more complicated. Macduff is eager for action and has risked all to stir Malcolm into reclaiming Scotland, but Malcolm is passive and suspicious. Where Macduff speaks with impulsive energy, Malcolm is more carefully logical in his language:

What I believe, I'll wail;
What know, believe; and what I can redress,
As I shall find the time to friend, I will. *(lines 8–10)*

He notes (with powerful unconscious irony at the expense of both speakers) that Macduff has been notably loyal to Macbeth and that he and his family remain unharmed. Malcolm suspects that Macduff may be one of Macbeth's agents, pretending to oppose the tyrant, whilst trying to lure Malcolm back to be destroyed in Scotland. If this were the case, then Macduff could be sure that his wife and children are safe.

Malcolm is honest enough to acknowledge that he simply doesn't know the truth, that it is impossible to read another man's mind, and that he may be insulting Macduff with his doubts. His 'doubts' conflict with the other's 'hopes'. He remains doubtful, since Macduff evades the argument about his family's safety by making a passionate lament for the state of Scotland. Ross was unable to answer the very similar argument put to him by Lady Macduff in the previous scene when she said, 'All is the fear, and nothing is the love'. It seems that the moral stature of Macbeth's opponents is too compromised for them to present a clear, untarnished challenge to his tyranny.

Malcolm confuses the situation further by declaring that the person succeeding Macbeth will be even more vicious. The claim seems so bizarre that Macduff has to ask whom Malcolm is speaking of. He answers that it is himself – and he launches into a catalogue of his vices: he claims to be guilty of sexual intemperance and avarice and to lack all the graces that are required in a king. Critics have noted that Malcolm's role in the play so far has been minimal and that the audience, as well as Macduff, should be puzzled by his words. Is this a genuine self-analysis or is it a trick? Malcolm's self-attack continues for 50 lines. Macduff regrets what he hears, but is prepared to tolerate the vices of lust and financial greed, since there are bound to be other qualities that make Malcolm more acceptable than Macbeth. But Malcolm declares:

> Nay, had I power, I should
> Pour the sweet milk of concord into hell,
> Uproar the universal peace, confound
> All unity on earth.   *(lines 97–100)*

The audience has heard sentiments like these before. In the middle of Act 4 Scene 1, when Macbeth confronted the Witches, he spoke of 'nature's germen' tumbling to destruction. He was prepared to tolerate – even to welcome – the principle of violent anarchy replacing a God-given order. Since Malcolm unconsciously recalls Macbeth's language, Shakespeare may be bringing their attitudes into a surprising comparison. Both leaders are prepared to manipulate the truth. Malcolm, with the support of King Edward the Confessor, is planning an invading force, but he here decides, for reasons not yet clear, to appear like a wicked man. Macbeth, on his route to evil, had to learn the skills of hypocrisy in order to appear good. Malcolm evidently knows the dangers of trusting appearances.

Macduff can tolerate no more, even in the interests of finding a legitimate king to replace Macbeth. He puts no further arguments to accept the catalogue of wickedness he hears. He laments, 'O Scotland, Scotland!' and then turns furiously on Malcolm, declaring him as unfit to live and unworthy of his saintly parents.

Malcolm is convinced by Macduff's passionate disappointment. Macduff's readiness to abandon his alliance with Malcolm seems to prove that his mission to England was genuine and that he is not in league with tyranny. In response, Malcolm tells how Macbeth has sent agents to England pretending loyalty to Malcolm in order to trap him. He denies the vices that he has just attributed to himself, and he announces that an English army led by Old Siward is ready to advance on Scotland.

After his headlong speech Malcolm asks Macduff why he is silent. This is made a deliberate comic effect in some productions. Macduff, now more relaxed, may smile at Malcolm's expecting him to adjust his responses so suddenly. On the other hand, Malcolm's deceit has disorientated Macduff, who now may be suffering shock at the sudden reversal. His lines seem non-committal:

> Such welcome and unwelcome things at once,
> 'Tis hard to reconcile. *(lines 138–9)*

Macduff's reply suggests that he is unsure about the alliance that Malcolm now offers. All the sins that Malcolm claimed for himself may be denied, but they can't be unsaid.

A doctor announces that a group of sick people are waiting for King Edward's healing touch. God has given him this power, which is passed down to his successors (a claim which King James did not believe). This short pause in the action has a symbolic value in contrasting the two kings: Macbeth dedicated to destruction, King Edward to healing. Such images of saintliness ('holy prayers', 'healing benediction', 'sundry blessings', 'full of grace') show that Malcolm is not just receiving protection from King Edward, but may be finding in him a father figure with qualities like those of Duncan. Some critics also claim that Shakespeare shows England not simply as a wholesome nation, the direct opposite of Macbeth's Scotland, but as one also afflicted by 'the evil', with a good king's constant vigilance needed to repel it.

Ross appears. Malcolm, not recognising him at first, makes a moral generalisation that people who should be friends are becoming strangers. Ross replies with a similar comment about Scotland: 'Almost afraid to know itself'. Violent sorrow has become the norm and distorts accepted certainties. Ross uses a moving image from nature, the fragility of plucked flowers, to show how brief and vulnerable human lives have become:

> The deadman's knell
> Is there scarce asked for who, and good men's lives
> Expire before the flowers in their caps,
> Dying or ere they sicken.   *(lines 172–5)*

Macduff enquires about his family, at which Ross's fluency deserts him. He evades the full truth, and chooses to equivocate, leading Macduff into the illusion that his family is 'at peace'. It is true that they were alive when he left, but the real irony of his remark is far more grim: they are 'at peace' in the sense that they, like Duncan, also lie at rest 'after life's fitful fever'.

Ross regains fluency as he speaks to Malcolm, promising that his appearance in Scotland would bring energy, purpose and great relief to its afflicted people. Malcolm replies with warm encouragement, and Ross steels himself to tell Macduff the appalling truth. He prepares Macduff for the worst, and then summarises the event with stark brevity:

> Your castle is surprised; your wife and babes
> Savagely slaughtered.   *(lines 206–7)*

Macduff absorbs the news, checks and questions it, as though unable to believe that Macbeth has found yet another dimension of inhuman savagery as to slaughter women and children. Ross repeats the cruel truth: 'Wife, children, servants, all / That could be found.' Malcolm urges Macduff to give vent to his grief and then to turn it into revenge. Macduff's reply, 'He has no children', can be interpreted in two different ways. Either he refers to the childless Macbeth, who therefore can't know what the death of a child means, or his remark is directed at Malcolm, rebuking his young inexperience for instantly suggesting that revenge will be a comfort in bereavement. Still Macduff seems to require clarity. In disbelief and urgent questioning, he locks on to the word 'all' and makes a tolling repetition of it:

> All my pretty ones?
> Did you say all? O hell-kite! All?
> What, all my pretty chickens and their dam
> At one fell swoop? *(lines 218–21)*

Malcolm tells Macduff to 'Dispute it like a man', unconsciously recalling earlier scenes between Macbeth and his wife about the nature of manliness. Here Malcolm, like Lady Macbeth, seems to suggest the stereotype of a true man is one who will take vigorous action. Malcolm, little more than a boy, presumes to instruct an experienced soldier about the nature of manhood. Macduff breaks out of his own grief to rebuke him: 'I shall do so; / But I must also feel it as a man'. He tells Malcolm a wiser truth about manliness: it is natural and healthy to take time to grieve and to focus on those who are lost. But Macduff is less clear about the role of heaven in this disaster:

> Did heaven look on,
> And would not take their part? *(lines 226–7)*

Several moral questions concern the behaviour of the three characters in this episode. Which is the more sensitive behaviour: Ross's silent presence or Malcolm's call to action? Is Malcolm genuinely trying to help Macduff to cope with his grief, or is he an opportunist urging him into the common cause against Macbeth? Can an audience react to Macduff with full sympathy, or is the response coloured by his wife's words in the last scene: that his fear and negligence allowed the disaster to happen?

The scene ends with Macduff hoping that he may meet Macbeth in one-to-one combat. Malcolm prepares to take leave of King Edward and will lead the army into Scotland. He sees the angels themselves ('the powers above') aiding the invasion, making it a crusade.

This scene is unusual in showing the effects of violence on the bereaved. Only one other scene attempts this: Act 2 Scene 3, when Malcolm and Donaldbain hear of their father's death. There the moment was brief and very undeveloped. Their grief ('not yet brewed', as Donaldbain put it) was swallowed up in the broader public horror that a king had been killed. There was hardly any focus on a father murdered. Malcolm then was as much concerned with his own safety as with losing his father. Macduff's suffering in Act 4 Scene 3 is more sensitive, personal and affecting.

However, the plot requires a continuing focus on public issues, and the ability of these two very different leaders, Malcolm and Macduff, to invade Scotland. Their success is not at all assured. Perhaps tensions have built up between them, and Shakespeare provides no evidence that heaven will support the virtuous. In his castle, Macbeth seems fully protected by the Witches' prophecies but Malcolm confidently ends Scene 3 with an ominous threat to Macbeth's security:

> Come, go we to the king; our power is ready;
> Our lack is nothing but our leave. Macbeth
> Is ripe for shaking, and the powers above
> Put on their instruments. Receive what cheer you may:
> The night is long that never finds the day.   *(lines 239–43)*

Act 4: Critical review

Act 4 leaves Macbeth's court, but his character and actions occupy everyone's thoughts. Scene 1 shows the Witches on their territory, where they mockingly treat Macbeth as their honoured guest. Scene 2 is in Macduff's castle, a domestic setting of mother and child, which Macbeth's murderers violate. Scene 3 leaves Scotland altogether. Malcolm and Macduff plan invasion, but Macbeth seems ominously present when Ross brings his shattering news.

Until Act 4 much of the play's violence has been shown more through the criminal than the victims, encouraging the audience to hold ambivalent attitudes towards Macbeth. They deplore what he is doing, but engage with his intimate thoughts and feelings. The effect of Scenes 2 and 3, when Macbeth is offstage for a long time, is to undermine that engagement, clearly presenting him as a tyrant who must be overthrown. Act 4 reveals the suffering and violence that people endure under Macbeth's regime in Scotland. Rumour and uncertainty add to the insecurity that pervades the country.

Some directors and critics find the long England scene difficult and incongruous. But it develops the character of Malcolm, who assesses the dangers and opportunities that he faces. He last appeared just after his father's murder, confused and planning to escape. Shakespeare now gives him the dramatic depth he needs as potential king and rescuer of Scotland, particularly in his controlled testing of Macduff and in his calculated self-denigration.

Macduff has already been portrayed as a strong character. Now Act 4 prepares him for combat with Macbeth. Like Malcolm, he is dedicated to the cause of Scotland and has suffered from Macbeth's violence. By the end of the act, Macduff's integrity has been tested and his resolve deepened by the need for personal revenge.

The three scenes in the act contain great dramatic range:
- Ritual: the Witches around their cauldron.
- Spectacle: the apparitions and the show of the eight kings.
- Domestic family life: Lady Macduff and her child.
- Horrific violation: the murders in Macduff's castle.
- Deception and moral complexity; Malcolm's testing of Macduff.
- Deep personal grief: Macduff hears of his family's slaughter.

Act 5 Scene 1

The previous scene ended with Malcolm's line, 'The night is long that never finds the day.' He used 'night' as a metaphor for tyranny and murder in Scotland. Act 5 returns to Scotland, to literal night-time and to one of its most private places: Lady Macbeth's chamber. A waiting gentlewoman, attending on the queen, has seen Lady Macbeth walking and behaving strangely in her sleep. A doctor has come to observe and to advise. He asks for more information but the Gentlewoman refuses to reveal the appalling secrets that she has heard. Her reticence may suggest that the details are too horrifying to report, or that she is frightened by her connection with the queen.

The Doctor acknowledges Lady Macbeth's plight to be 'A great perturbation in nature', an image which recalls the turmoil in the natural world described in Act 2 Scene 4. More specifically, the concern about disturbed sleep reminds the audience of the moments just after King Duncan's murder. Then, Macbeth spoke obsessively of murdering sleep ('Balm of hurt minds'), but his wife dismissed his anxiety as 'brain-sickly'. It is now ironic that Lady Macbeth has become sick in her mind and is suffering sleeplessness.

Lady Macbeth appears carrying a taper, a fragile source of light, perhaps symbolic of her tentative hold on sanity. The Doctor and Gentlewoman watch and comment, first on the light, which Lady Macbeth insists on having beside her. The Doctor notices the obsessive rubbing of her hands, trying to erase 'a spot', which her open eyes cannot see because 'their sense are shut'. The Doctor prepares to note down a record of her words. The case is unique and he needs to remember the details accurately. Lady Macbeth cannot erase the spot, however hard she tries. She remembers fragments from the past:

- the sounds of a bell or clock ('One, two.')
- comments she made to Macbeth when planning Duncan's murder
- seeing the bloodstained body of Duncan as she returned the daggers
- Lady Macduff's murder ('The Thane of Fife had a wife.')
- the banquet at which Macbeth saw Banquo's ghost
- the urgent noise of Macduff knocking on the gate

Most hauntingly of all, she is absorbed by the illusion of her bloodstained hand:

> Here's the smell of the blood still; all the perfumes of Arabia
> will not sweeten this little hand.   *(lines 42–3)*

Ever since Pontius Pilate washed his hands, so refusing to accept any part in the death of Jesus, the image of blood on the hands has symbolised guilt. Lady Macbeth's actions here are especially ironic in view of her comment to Macbeth in Act 2 Scene 2: 'A little water clears us of this deed. / How easy is it then!' There was real blood then on Macbeth's hand: now there is the illusion of blood on hers. As she leaves she asks him to take her hand, a gesture both of need and complicity. But Macbeth is not there.

The Doctor ends the scene with a choric summary. As with Macbeth and his wife, so with their observers: the horror goes inwards, deep into the mind. The Doctor speaks of disorder in nature and 'infected minds', suggesting that his skills as a physician are inadequate: Lady Macbeth needs psychological and spiritual help. His last line, 'I think, but dare not speak', implies that, like the Gentlewoman, he will be safer if he remains silent.

The power of the scene means that actors who play Lady Macbeth are often judged and remembered for their ability to move an audience. The dramatic intensity of her sleepwalking is increased by the horror and fear felt by the onstage 'audience', the Doctor and Gentlewoman, and by the shocking fragility of a once-powerful queen. Lady Macbeth's broken language, moving without control over fragments of the past, contrasts oddly with the precision and focus of her actions. The scene also foreshadows modern psychoanalytic concern with dreams and the workings of the unconscious mind.

Act 5 Scene 2

The action moves from the privacy of Lady Macbeth's chamber to a crowded scene of a Scottish army opposed to Macbeth. It is waiting for the English army to join them. Their appearance begins to fulfil the promises for revival in Scotland.

Menteith, Angus and Caithness act more as commentators than as individualised characters. They give information about the English leaders, the older and young Siward, and they tell of an imminent meeting at Birnam Wood. They speak of very young men gathering against Macbeth, perhaps suggesting the moral idealism for a new Scotland. The centre of this short scene depicts Macbeth through a mixture of fact and guesses. No one mentions his name: he is simply 'the tyrant'. His mental state is hard to define:

> Some say he's mad; others that lesser hate him
> Do call it valiant fury   *(lines 13–14)*

Menteith guesses at Macbeth's inner disturbance in words that might also describe Lady Macbeth in the previous scene:

> Who then shall blame
> His pestered senses to recoil and start,
> When all that is within him does condemn
> Itself for being there?   *(lines 22–5)*

The lines recall the erratic bursts of rage that the guests saw at the banquet, but more crucially describe an inner conflict and self-hatred so disturbing that Macbeth's very identity seems threatened.

Shakespeare uses some of the play's familiar images to describe Macbeth and his opponents. Images of clothes are expressed in buckling 'the belt of rule' and 'a giant's robe' too large for 'a dwarfish thief'. Sickness recurs as a 'distempered cause' and the English army as 'med'cine' to purge 'the sickly weal'. Lennox's final optimistic image is of natural growth: their drops of blood will give nourishing dew to the flower (Malcolm), but will drown the weeds (Macbeth).

Act 5 Scene 3

'Bring me no more reports, let them fly all'. Macbeth's first line suggests that he is receiving constant and depressing intelligence. He defies and rejects these reports and tries to reassure himself with the prophecies that the Witches gave him in Act 4. He determines never to 'shake with fear', and sneers at the terrified servant who has brought news of the English army. Many productions show Macbeth's random violence by having him assault the servant; in one he gashed the servant's face when telling him to 'over-red thy fear'.

He sinks into a brief, unwavering acknowledgement of his empty life. Though the Doctor is present, Macbeth's lines (22–8) may be played as a soliloquy, which some critics judge the most bleak and truthful of his confessions. There is great weariness in the words, 'I have lived long enough.' He recalls the ideals that all men share, but which are denied to him:

> And that which should accompany old age,
> As honour, love, obedience, troops of friends,
> I must not look to have   *(lines 24–6)*

In some performances 'I must not look to have' is spoken as an objective judgement, as though Macbeth is trying to be scrupulously accurate in defining his plight, rather than clouding it with anger, bitterness or self-pity. The ideals of old age are replaced by curses, admittedly 'not loud but deep'. He describes his servants' apparent respect as 'mouth-honour', a seemingly clumsy word that conveys their awkward hypocrisy towards him.

Seyton enters to confirm the desperate news and to attend to Macbeth's armour. Some productions suggest that he is the only servant who remains loyal and useful to Macbeth. He may already have appeared as the Third Murderer at the death of Banquo and in Lady Macduff's castle. Sometimes his name is pronounced 'Satan', further defining this place as the castle of hell.

Macbeth's query to the Doctor about 'your patient' refers to Lady Macbeth, but he does not mention her by name, nor does he express any sense of love or lost companionship. Meanwhile Seyton is helping Macbeth with his armour, and in some productions his silent presence creates a sinister effect. Macbeth behaves erratically. At first he wants his armour on, then he wants it to be pulled off. When the Doctor describes Lady Macbeth's 'thick-coming fancies', Macbeth demands that they be cured. Perhaps he feels that the Doctor has come too close to seeing what afflicts both husband and wife and so reacts by accusing him of incompetence. Perhaps he is pleading for what he knows to be impossible: a return to mental health:

> Canst thou not minister to a mind diseased,
> Pluck from the memory a rooted sorrow,
> Raze out the written troubles of the brain,
> And with some sweet oblivious antidote
> Cleanse the stuffed bosom of that perilous stuff
> Which weighs upon the heart?   *(lines 41–6)*

The rapid action of the play pauses. Macbeth seems to reflect longingly on the far-away vision of calmer times, especially in the stretched-out phrase, 'sweet oblivious antidote'. After the gentle word 'minister', the sharper verbs – 'Pluck', 'Raze', 'Cleanse' – each at the beginning of a line, emphasise Macbeth's wish for a new start. But he realises it is impossible to go back, just as he recognised after the banquet when he imagined wading through a river of blood. Perhaps he tries to clear the wish from his mind with a sardonic joke: he suggests that the Doctor could heal the sickness of Scotland by testing its urine ('cast / The water of my land'). Humour can sometimes be a temporary respite from despair, but here Macbeth seems to use it to express how acutely he recognises reality.

The Doctor says little: conversation with Macbeth is full of potential dangers. He does not tell of what he overheard from Lady Macbeth in her sleepwalking. It is only after Macbeth's swaggering exit line that he confesses to the audience his real feeling expressing how everyone feels trapped by Macbeth's tyranny and is waiting for release:

> Were I from Dunsinane away and clear,
> Profit again should hardly draw me here. *(lines 62–3)*

Act 5 Scene 4

The invading soldiers move nearer to their goal. The scene's main purpose is to frustrate Macbeth's trust in the prophecy he recalled only four lines earlier: that he can never be defeated until the wood advances on the castle. Malcolm relies on secrecy and surprise: he orders the soldiers to conceal their numbers by camouflaging themselves with branches cut from Birnam Wood.

The leaders plan their assault with methodical care. Malcolm judges accurately that Macbeth is forced to remain in his fortified castle because so many soldiers have deserted. Only compulsion keeps a few men with him, and their morale is low. Macduff and Siward end the scene by relying on 'Industrious soldiership' and by not becoming over-confident about victory. Their shrewd realism is very different from Macbeth's bravado.

Act 5 Scene 5

At Dunsinane Castle Macbeth has not yet seen the trees moving, and he relies on aggressive display: 'Hang out our banners on the outward walls'. He appears to despise the enemy's chances, but resents his own deserters who have fled to join Malcolm. He believes that with his full army he could have beaten the invaders in open battle.

The sound of women lamenting would unnerve a normal man, but Macbeth finds it hard to remember 'the taste of fears'. Seyton's report that the queen is dead evokes the play's most famous soliloquy. After touching on 'She' in the first line, Macbeth says nothing more of Lady Macbeth nor of his relationship with her. They have moved inexorably apart.

Macbeth speaks of time past, present and future and of how brief and fragile he finds human life. 'Tomorrow, and tomorrow, and tomorrow' with its featureless repetition leads to further repetition: 'from day to day / To the last syllable of recorded time'. Human beings record time in order to give significance to their lives and events, but Macbeth finds this wearyingly pointless. His thought moves from 'tomorrow' to 'to day' to the 'yesterdays' which give no help other than lighting the way to 'dusty death'. It is followed by the image of a 'brief candle'. Perhaps Shakespeare is recalling Lady Macbeth's flickering taper in her sleepwalking scene.

> Out, out, brief candle,
> Life's but a walking shadow, a poor player
> That struts and frets his hour upon the stage
> And then is heard no more. It is a tale
> Told by an idiot, full of sound and fury
> Signifying nothing.   *(lines 22–7)*

The 'brief candle' symbolises life which may even be less than a flickering light: a mere 'shadow'. In Shakespeare's time, 'shadow' was often used as a metaphor for an actor (or 'player' as he was then called). Macbeth's train of thought has led him from measuring time, to light, to shadow, to a player who asserts himself merely for 'his hour'. The comparison of life on earth to a stage and actors was very common both in Shakespeare's writing and in plays of his time. The Spanish Renaissance playwright, Calderon, used it as the title of one of his greatest plays: *The World's Great Stage*.

The metaphor of the stage emphasises Macbeth's despair and misplaced energies. The empty posturing suggested in the stunted verbs 'struts' and 'frets' may suggest how he has played the role of king. It has been a brief experience, it will be 'heard no more', and it is so absurd that he describes it as 'a tale / Told by an idiot'. Macbeth has become the target of his own sardonic irony. Part of Macbeth's tragedy is that he is aware of his life's emptiness. His speech ends with two words that, together, embody an ironic contradiction: 'Signifying' is formal, polysyllabic and seems to promise something significant to follow; but then there is 'nothing'.

The play's action gains new energy with the Messenger's arrival. He has seen Birnam Wood moving towards Dunsinane. Macbeth's response is a now-typical mixture of threat, bravado and weariness. He is aware of being manipulated:

> I pull in resolution and begin
> To doubt th'equivocation of the fiend
> That lies like truth.   *(lines 41–3)*

'That lies like truth' recalls two motif lines from Act I which also suggest equivocation: 'Fair is foul, and foul is fair'; 'nothing is, / But what is not.' Macbeth recognises how his prospects and sense of self-worth have shrunk, but he hurries out to battle determined to end his life like a soldier:

> At least we'll die with harness on our back.   *(line 51)*

Act 5 Scenes 6 and 7

The remaining scenes all dramatise the battle, and most productions will run them together in rapid succession. In Scene 6 Malcolm orders his army to throw down their branches 'And show like those you are.' He gives crisp military orders and the trumpets announce his challenge to Macbeth. His manoeuvre answers the deceit Macbeth has needed to survive as a tyrant. However, there is a rich irony in the device. Malcolm is, in effect, clothing his soldiers with Nature's greenery, the sign of renewing life. In one sense, this predicts the restoration of peace and growth. But it is also a trick, and the soldiers will soon cast the lopped trees to the ground and show themselves for what they are: a destructive force.

Scene 7 is in the castle or perhaps just outside it. Macbeth recognises he is trapped: 'They have tied me to a stake; I cannot fly'. He is reduced to being chained like a bear and must fight against his first opponent, Young Siward. He relies on the terrifying implications of his name – the word 'Macbeth' has become a curse from hell – and on supernatural help. His rapid slaughter of Young Siward seems to prove that he is invulnerable:

> But swords I smile at, weapons laugh to scorn,
> Brandished by man that's of a woman born.   *(lines 13–14)*

Macduff enters, searching for Macbeth. He too labels him as 'Tyrant', ignoring other opponents, who are irrelevant to his purpose of revenge. Siward announces an easy victory: his army has taken the castle, helped by Macbeth's soldiers who have changed sides. The rapid entrances and exits emphasise the flow of action that leads inevitably to Macbeth's defeat.

Act 5 Scene 8

> Why should I play the Roman fool and die
> On mine own sword? Whiles I see lives, the gashes
> Do better upon them.   *(lines 1–3)*

Although the main battle appears to be over, Macbeth remains in isolated defiance. It was a sign of honour in Roman soldiers (like Brutus in *Julius Caesar*) to commit suicide when all was lost. Macbeth here equates this type of honour with folly and aims to continue his habit of violence against others.

He hears a voice from behind him and turns to face Macduff. They exchange very few words. Macduff declares, 'My voice is in my sword', but when they pause for breath with the conflict apparently inconclusive, Macbeth boasts of his 'charmèd life'. He again uses the phrase 'To one of woman born', to which he has clung like a talisman. Macduff declares the magic to be impotent:

> Despair thy charm,
> And let the angel whom thou still hast served
> Tell thee, Macduff was from his mother's womb
> Untimely ripped.   *(lines 13–16)*

Macduff was born by Caesarian section. Though 'Untimely ripped' may seem a frightening image, it is appropriate in describing the birth of an avenger and also for this moment of facing Macbeth as he is about to fulfil his destiny. The revelation destroys Macbeth's confidence and he is forced to recognise that he has been duped and mocked:

> And be these juggling fiends no more believed
> That palter with us in a double sense,
> That keep the word of promise to our ear
> And break it to our hope.   *(lines 19–22)*

These lines virtually define equivocation. The Witches, or their masters who control destiny, have proved more skilful equivocators than Macbeth or anyone else. For a moment Macbeth is prepared to submit. But when Macduff insults him with 'coward', followed by the threat to exhibit him as 'monster' and 'tyrant', he immediately finds the energy to 'try the last'. Some critics find in Macbeth's final outburst a great soldier's courage and an impressive pride in refusing to become a captive freak in Malcolm's triumph. Others see it merely as an animal instinct in a man who has despaired of human life.

Act 5 Scene 9

> I would the friends we miss were safe arrived.   *(line 1)*

The final scene begins with Malcolm's concern for the safety of his own men, followed by Siward's brusque comment, 'Some must go off.' The remark is that of a tough veteran, used to setbacks and sorrow, but immediately he has to face the loss of his own son. Ross, for the second time, brings news of bereavement to a father and Siward accepts it without apparent emotion. His question simply concerns honour: was his son facing the enemy when he died? Ross and Malcolm try to pay the young man the respect of their grief, but the father feels that a soldier's respect is better shown in terse acceptance:

> They say he parted well and paid his score,
> And so God be with him.   *(lines 19–20)*

Any individual, however close and loved, matters less than a soldier's code of honour and the public cause: the rescue of Scotland.

Believing this, Siward finds comfort in the arrival of Macduff, carrying Macbeth's severed head. Macduff's words are also totally concerned with the public good, not with his own grief nor his personal revenge:

> Hail, king, for so thou art. Behold where stands
> Th'usurper's cursèd head. The time is free.   *(lines 21–2)*

In saying 'for so thou art', he may be stressing Malcolm's legitimacy as king, contrasting with the 'usurper'. He may also be urging the silent younger man into accepting the reality and the responsibilities of his new role. Some productions show all of the characters in a state of shock, partly because of their success and partly because of the grim trophy of Macbeth's bleeding head. 'The time is free' stands as an isolated brief sentence, perhaps because no one can fully imagine freedom from terror after such tyranny. Macduff must urge them into accepting it. He has fulfilled the role that was symbolically predicted in Act 2 when he knocked on the gate of 'Hell Castle'. He takes the lead in this first acknowledgement of freedom, and then hands over the leadership to Malcolm, asking for other voices to share in his homage to the new king.

Malcolm's final speech has evoked varied responses from critics. A liberal humanist view declares that order has been restored, that the disease of Scotland has been purged away, and that Malcolm (benefiting from King Edward as tutor) will restore the nation's health and follow his father's holy life. Some directors celebrate this optimism with stage effects, such as loud cheering, raising Malcolm high on their shields, and even an impromptu coronation.

Wilbur Sanders challenges this interpretation: he feels that, whereas Duncan was 'the lost possibility', Malcolm is the 'diminished necessity'. Words and phrases such as 'reckon', 'make us even', 'what needful else', 'We will perform in measure, time, and place' all may suggest a coolness, very different from Duncan's humanity and warm regard for his subjects. Malcolm may appear wary and bureaucratic, but his caution is justified because Macbeth's evil tyranny has removed for ever the old Scotland. If virtue is to exist in the future it must be of a different type: more austere and watchful.

In his first appointments Malcolm stresses that new times lie ahead:

> My thanes and kinsmen,
> Henceforth be earls, the first that ever Scotland
> In such an honour named.   *(lines 29–31)*

Shakespeare may here be alluding to King James's decision at the start of his reign to reward his supporters with earldoms. It is policy in a leader both to reward and to promise new opportunities, but some critics recall Duncan's gift of honours. Macbeth's appointment as Thane of Cawdor encouraged illicit ambition, leading to murder and tyranny. It may be that Malcolm is unwittingly encouraging the cycle to continue. He may even be seen as the currently successful warlord, one among many who use force and cunning to gain power, and who may in his turn be overthrown.

This final speech sounds both assertive and guarded, and in one production Lennox handed Malcolm a prepared script for the leader's formal reading. Malcolm very properly promises to recall friends from abroad and to punish criminals. But his 'what needful else' and the reference to rumours about Lady Macbeth's possible suicide may seem to continue the play's equivocation. The phrase 'as 'tis thought' recalls 'reports', 'whisperings', 'I hear it by the way', and other moments of uncertainty. In some productions the victors, with barely the energy to cheer, receive their earldoms with unease, and make their exits unsure about the new hierarchy.

Some directors have the Witches present at these final moments. Sometimes they pick at Macbeth's corpse, the victim they enticed to disaster. Sometimes they attend on Malcolm, so marking him out also as potential victim, even as he invites his supporters 'to see us crowned at Scone'. In Polanski's film Donaldbain returns to the place where Macbeth and Banquo met the Witches, suggesting that he too is a warlord soon to challenge for power.

Some critics feel that such explicit interpolations spoil the ambiguity of Shakespeare's ending, which leaves the future uncertain. Many productions show the terrifying past, symbolised by Macbeth's severed head, to be more powerful than either the present victory or future plans. Malcolm's brief and formal speech is dwarfed by the image of bloody mutilation and the dead Macbeth's grimace that can suggest either triumph or defeat.

Act 5: Critical review

The dramatic construction of Act 5 uses short scenes alternating between Macbeth's castle and the approaching army from England. Some productions keep both groups onstage throughout after Scene 2 and give the necessary focus on each group through lighting changes. The contrast of scene with scene is a type of antithesis, which is so strongly present in the play's language.

There is further contrast in the opponents' behaviour. Macbeth is erratic but increasingly full of bravado and violence at the prospect of battle. Malcolm and his supporters are restrained in expressing their determination. They believe in the justice of their cause, but do not take success for granted.

In Act 4 Lady Macbeth did not appear, nor was she mentioned. Now her appearance in Scene 1 is startling. The assertive confidence of Acts 1 and 2 has gone and she has suffered a severe mental breakdown. Act 3 suggested her growing separation from Macbeth, and now Act 5 shows their relationship severed. They have reacted to isolation very differently. Whereas she once considered him weak, he has now found strength to fight on. She has totally withdrawn and suffers exhausting nightmares from her guilt at 'what's done'.

Macbeth is brought to realise that each of the Witches' prophecies, apparently so encouraging, is fulfilled in a way that shatters his confidence. He once terrorised others: now he feels he is the plaything of unknown powers that have mocked and misled him. His slaying by Macduff is dramatically appropriate:

- Macduff's knocking on the gate in Act 2, with its allusion to *The Harrowing of Hell*, singled him out as avenger and rescuer.
- The murder of Macduff's family is cruel and gratuitous and his reaction is the play's strongest expression of grief.
- Macbeth had clung most strongly to the prophecy that he could not be defeated by one 'of woman born'. He did not foresee the strange way in which Macduff would fulfil this prophecy.

Malcolm ends the play promising to reward his followers and rebuild Scotland, but Shakespeare's dramatic skill enables the ending to be played in ways which predict either peace or tyranny ahead.

Contexts

This section identifies the contexts from which *Macbeth* emerged: the wide range of different influences which fostered the creativity of Shakespeare as he wrote the play.

What did Shakespeare write?

Sometime around 1606, Shakespeare, already an experienced and popular playwright, wrote *Macbeth*. It may have been first performed in July or August by The King's Men, Shakespeare's company, for King James and his guest, King Christian IV of Denmark. The Scottish King James had ruled in England for three years, and the alliance of the two countries made 'the Scottish play' topical. Shakespeare also must have known of James's interest in witchcraft. In addition, *Macbeth* refers to the hanging of traitors and possibly to the gunpowder plot of 1605. The play's concern with equivocation may reflect the well-known argument presented by one of the plot's conspirators, the Jesuit Father Garnet, who asserted that equivocating (lying) was justified. He was executed in May 1606 and some scholars argue the play was written shortly afterwards.

What was the play that Shakespeare wrote and his audiences heard? No one knows for certain because the original manuscript has not survived, nor was the play published in his lifetime. *Macbeth* appeared for the first time in 1623, seven years after Shakespeare's death. It was published in the volume known as the First Folio (a collection of 36 of his plays). It is supposed that the printers used a theatre prompt book or a copy of it.

Today all editions of *Macbeth* are based on that 1623 version. But the edition of the play you are using will vary in many minor respects from other editions. That is because, although every editor of the play uses the Folio version, each one makes many different judgements about spelling, punctuation, stage directions, scene locations and other features.

So even though the text of *Macbeth* is not entirely stable, this is no cause for dismay, but rather an opportunity to think about how differences affect what actually happens in performance. Every production, on stage, film, radio or TV, cuts, adapts and amends the text to present its own unique version of *Macbeth*. This Guide follows the New Cambridge edition of the play (also used in Cambridge School Shakespeare).

What did Shakespeare read?

Shakespeare, like many contemporary playwrights, gained much of his source material from history books written in Queen Elizabeth's reign. Virtually all of these books used history to support the Tudor dynasty, which began with the reign of Henry VII in 1485. As he wrote *Macbeth*, Shakespeare had at his side a history book he had frequently used before as inspiration for his English History plays: *Holinshed's Chronicles*. In 1587 Raphael Holinshed published the second edition of his huge work, *Chronicles of England, Scotland and Ireland*. This book was part of a greater intention, never completed, a 'cosmography of the whole world including the histories of every known nation', beginning with the sons of Noah. Three stories in Holinshed's history fired Shakespeare's imagination as he wrote *Macbeth*:

1. King Duff was murdered by a trusted nobleman, Donwald, whose wife provided pressure and practical advice, including a feast to get his guards drunk. The king's corpse was hidden in a river bed, and Scotland was afflicted with darkness and strange events until there was a proper burial.

2. King Kenneth murdered Duff's son to ensure his own son's succession. He was tormented by a voice at night that disturbed his sleep and threatened his future.

3. Macbeth's career, the influence of his ambitious wife, the murder of Duncan and Banquo, Malcolm's testing of Macduff, and the advance of Birnam Wood to Dunsinane Castle. This is the story that provides the framework and most of the events for Shakespeare's play.

Shakespeare was interested in political manoeuvres and the exercise of power. Holinshed gave him not only important events, but also information about characters and motives. From even the slightest hints, Shakespeare was able to dramatise the psychological tensions within kings and other public figures, especially through the interplay of their private and public lives. His writing avoids being simply didactic; it raises issues and asks questions without overt commitment to any particular political view. To create vibrant drama, Shakespeare altered what he read in Holinshed. Here are some of his changes:

- Shakespeare makes Duncan a respected king. Holinshed presents him as ineffectual and negligent, giving Macdonald some justification for his rebellion.
- Shakespeare conflates two battles (Macdonald's rebellion and Sweno's invasion) into the one reported by the Captain.
- Macbeth commits the murder himself, whereas Donwald orders his servants to kill King Duff and then murders them.
- Shakespeare's Macbeth is a tyrant as soon as he becomes king, whereas Holinshed tells of ten years of effective rule and important reforms.
- Shakespeare invents the banquet scene with Banquo's ghost, and Macbeth's visit to the Witches in Act 4 Scene 1, where he sees the three apparitions and the show of Banquo and the eight kings. None of this appears in Holinshed.
- Holinshed described Banquo as Macbeth's accomplice. Shakespeare's Banquo remains comparatively independent and guiltless.
- Shakespeare gives fewer political and military details than appear in Holinshed, so that greater focus can fall on Duncan's murder, which dominates Act 2 and then resonates through the play.
- Shakespeare greatly increases the importance of the Witches, so raising questions about the supernatural, free will and the nature of evil.

Shakespeare's most significant changes affect the two main characters. He gives audiences full access to Macbeth's tortured inner life. His Macbeth is often hesitant in the first half of the play; he is troubled in his conscience and expresses conflict and anguish in his soliloquies. Holinshed writes very little about the relationship between Macbeth and his wife, but Shakespeare builds up a close affection and sexual bond, before portraying their growing separation from Act 3 onwards. Shakespeare gives Lady Macbeth far more prominence. His creativity was stirred by just a few lines in Holinshed: she 'was very ambitious, burning in unquenchable desire to bear the name of queen'. From this, Shakespeare invents her invocation to the spirits in Act 1 Scene 5 and her persuasion of Macbeth, so that the conspiracy to murder becomes a combination of male and female as well as of two different temperaments. Lady

Macbeth's sleepwalking is also Shakespeare's invention, and powerfully expresses her emotional breakdown.

Drama: the influence of genre

Shakespeare saw and read different types of play, both those written in his lifetime and also those from earlier times that had become part of England's theatrical heritage. He borrowed and adapted much of this dramatic material to enrich his own writing. *Macbeth* owes much to the genres of miracle and morality plays, tragedy and masque.

Miracle plays

Miracle plays were a popular form of entertainment and instruction throughout the Middle Ages. They were dramatised stories from the Bible, originally staged inside churches, but as they became popular and more demanding in their staging and effects, they were performed in the open air. The plays covered an immense range of biblical history: the tragic fall of Lucifer, Adam's disobedience, God's incarnation and Christ redeeming mankind, and the Last Judgement. The plays were performed in groups (or cycles) and evoked a wide range of moods and audience response. Wicked characters, such as Cain, Herod and Christ's persecutors, often became raucous and farcical, so that absurdity in their presentation contrasted with the terror of their roles in the stories.

The critic Glynne Wickham has argued that the appearance of the Porter in Act 2 Scene 3 is based on a traditional play called *The Harrowing of Hell* from a cycle of miracle plays. It dramatises hell as a castle, often with a dragon's mouth as its entrance. After his crucifixion, Christ descends to hell, beats on the gate and requires Satan to release all the souls of patriarchs and prophets he has imprisoned there. The porter who guards the gate is named Rybald, from which the word 'ribald' derives, meaning coarse, vulgar and scurrilous. When Christ makes his demand, thunder, screams and groans are heard in the depths of Hell Castle.

Shakespeare uses several aspects of this miracle play in *Macbeth*. The Porter jokes in ribald language and, as he struggles through his hangover, imagines that he is the porter of hell-gate. Lennox, appearing shortly afterwards, tells of 'Lamentings heard i'th'air', ironically not knowing that Macbeth is turning his castle and the whole of Scotland into a type of hell. Macduff plays a dominant role in the scene. It is he that beats on the gate and he is the first to discover the murder. In Act 4 he suffers the appalling loss of his family and temporarily questions the role of heaven, but then commits himself to 'gentle heavens' to lead him in the battle against evil. In Act 5 he enters the castle again, but this time as the redeemer of Scotland who has killed the devil–tyrant and so, symbolically, leads the people from darkness into light.

Morality plays

Shakespeare expresses the conflict between good and evil more starkly in *Macbeth* than in any of his other tragedies. That conflict was prominent in morality plays, a type of drama developed in the late thirteenth century and still performed in 1600. The morality play began as part of Church instruction, a type of dramatised sermon. Moral issues faced by ordinary people were expressed through personified figures whose names declared a single trait, such as Avarice, Poverty, Sloth, Justice, Temperance. Such 'characters' were not portrayed as believable human beings; instead they demonstrated the pressures on a single central figure (Mankind or Everyman), whose soul became the battleground on which good and evil fought for supremacy.

Macbeth is far more sophisticated than a morality play and Macbeth is far more complex than the traditional figures of Mankind and Everyman. But the play has similar features: a man highly valued in his community is tempted by a great prize. It dramatises the battle of his conscience against his wife and the Witches' enticing suggestions. His conscience loses, Macbeth is damned, and from Act 3 onwards the play moves away from the genre of morality play and explores the nature of a living damnation.

Morality plays became part of popular entertainment. Since evil makes more impact on stage than goodness, devils and 'Vice' figures became lively, charismatic and often comic. These characters provided opportunities for hyperbolic language, colourful costume, violence and slapstick. Shakespeare's Porter is not a villain, but is an example of a comic character brought into a serious context and whose language and concerns are those of ordinary people: he does not like being woken up, he is drunk and he explains at some length how drink defeats a man.

Macbeth also includes more subtle comedy in the forms of irony and absurdity. When he sees the Ghost in the banquet scene, Macbeth complains that times have changed and now dead men do not remain dead; when hearing of Macduff's unusual birth, he lashes out angrily at how he has been tricked: 'And be these juggling fiends no more believed'. The tyrant becoming a victim is the subject matter of farce, typical of what could happen to devils and villains in a morality play. Irony, farce and very black comedy are strands of the complex mixture in *Macbeth*, which Shakespeare drew from earlier theatre.

Tragedy

Tragedy was written to instruct as well as to entertain. It taught audiences lessons about ambition, duty, loyalty and treachery, virtues and vices that can be made even more vivid and powerful in a high political context where the fates of nations, as well as individuals, are at stake. Tragedies were popular in Shakespeare's England. They dramatised great civil disasters and falls from power of kings, princes and military leaders, which affected the fortunes of states and nations. They contained assassination, bloodshed and revenge. In the popular genre now known as revenge tragedy, the action of the play is driven by the hero's plan to avenge some great wrong committed against him or his family. Usually he is unable to find justice at court. His plan is often intricate and secretive, requiring the playwright to construct a complicated plot. Shakespeare's major revenge tragedies are *Hamlet* and *Titus Andronicus*, but there are elements of the genre in *Macbeth*. Malcolm and Macduff can be seen as avengers in that both suffered family losses at Macbeth's hand and both wish to restore Scotland to health and good order. But Shakespeare put greater focus on Macbeth, especially on the struggles within his conscience and imagination, and so the play partially uses, rather than follows, the tradition of Elizabethan and Jacobean revenge tragedy.

A strong influence on the development of Elizabethan tragedy was the Roman playwright, Seneca (4 BC–AD 65). A collection of his tragedies, based on stories from Greek mythology, was published in 1581. Seneca's plays were enjoyed on the popular stage for their theatrical qualities, and they influenced many playwrights, including Shakespeare. The critic A C Bradley finds many parallels between Seneca and *Macbeth*, especially in the language of Macbeth's speech in 'Will all great Neptune's ocean . . .' (Act 2 Scene 2, line 63). Other features of *Macbeth* typically found in Senecan tragedy include:

- soliloquy
- exaggerated rhetoric
- ghosts, witches, magic
- violent events
- wrongs avenged
- moral statements

Another major influence on Shakespeare's dramatic creativity was Christopher Marlowe (1564–93). His career as a playwright coincided with Shakespeare's early work. He made a powerful impact with *Tamburlaine the Great*, the story of a Scythian shepherd whose colossal ambition and ruthless crushing of opponents gave him unrivalled power. Tamburlaine sees himself on a level with the gods, but at his death he is forced to accept the limits of his human mortality. In his prologue to the play Marlowe invites the audience to

> View but his picture in this tragic glass
> And then applaud his fortunes as you please.

Perhaps 'as you please' invites ambivalent responses: it is possible for audiences to admire assertive energy, but also to deplore the hero's crimes. Some critics find this ambivalence in Shakespeare's portrayal of Macbeth.

Marlowe's plays have often been seen as a turning point in the development of English tragedy. His heroes have been described as 'over-reachers', not bound by old conventions or religious beliefs. *Doctor Faustus* is the tragedy of a fine scholar, able to master all branches of knowledge, but so intellectually restless that he finally explores black magic. He makes a contract with the devil, who will give him unlimited earthly power and pleasure in return for Faustus' soul at the end of 24 years.

Doctor Faustus was written 14 years before *Macbeth*, and critics have often compared and contrasted the two. Both heroes are highly gifted and begin their careers honoured in their societies. Both are restlessly ambitious, and they stray beyond what is permissible in the mortal world and engage with magic and evil. Even though audiences are excited by the sense of danger, they also recognise the waste of potential as both Faustus and Macbeth misuse their gifts. Both suffer guilt and violent mental conflicts between their impulses towards good and evil.

Masque

The masque was primarily a Jacobean form that combined theatrical action, spectacle, music and elaborate tribute to important guests, expensively staged for the king's court. It was particularly developed by Shakespeare's contemporaries Ben Jonson and Inigo Jones. A typical masque would promote the ideology of royalty. King James's personal frailties (such as avarice, gluttony, lack of charisma) were ignored in the masque's function to celebrate the monarch as embodying order and harmony and banishing evil. Masques often included anti-masques, which presented the dangerous power of evil. For example, Jonson's *Masque of Queens* (1609) opened with witches performing their rites in a gloomy setting.

Macbeth uses the masque tradition in Act 4 Scene 1, which has been interpreted as a parody of a court masque. The Witches prepare for their royal guest and then 'entertain' him with apparently reassuring prophecies. In some productions they also feed him with the ingredients of their cauldron. They show him a processional pageant of Banquo's descendants, and when this vision appals him, they pretend concern: 'But why / Stands Macbeth thus amazedly?' To cheer his spirits and to fulfil their duties as 'court' entertainers, they offer him a dance (their 'antic round'). The scene gains its unsettling humour from paradox: the Witches play the roles of the king's servants or paid entertainers, but in a far more important sense they are his masters and manipulators. They know that since Act 1 they have fed him with temptations to which he has always succumbed.

What was Shakespeare's England like?

Like all writers, Shakespeare reflected in his plays the world he knew. Audiences watching *Macbeth* would recognise aspects of their own time and country. Shakespeare was not concerned with strict historical accuracy and setting, and *Macbeth* draws images from everyday experience, and from the customs and preoccupations of Jacobean England. Hearing them, Shakespeare's original audiences could respond at different levels. Today, insight into such contexts can similarly enrich your experience of the drama, enabling you to appreciate more extended possibilities of meaning. For example, some critics believe that Shakespeare wrote *Macbeth* partly as a tribute to King James, already king of Scotland, who became king of England in 1603 after Queen Elizabeth's death. Several aspects of the play have been taken to support this view:

- King James made a special study of witchcraft. His book, *Demonologie*, contains beliefs and detailed practices which also appear in *Macbeth*.
- In Act 4 the Witches show Macbeth a pageant of eight kings. Banquo gestures to them as his descendants. King James claimed direct descent from Banquo and to be the ninth king. There is a story that the eighth king carried a 'glass' (mirror) and focused it on James, who was watching the play.
- As a Protestant king, James deplored Catholic practices. It is thought that the Porter's talk of 'an equivocator' refers to a Catholic priest, Henry Garnet, who was accused in 1606 of being involved in the gunpowder plot. He committed perjury but claimed the right to equivocate (to mislead the court without technically lying). In *Macbeth* equivocation is associated with evil and is practised by the Witches and their 'masters'.
- In 1605 King James and Parliament escaped destruction when the gunpowder plot was discovered. A medal was struck to commemorate the discovery; it showed a snake concealed by flowers. In their first scene Lady Macbeth urges her husband into deceitful concealment: 'look like th'innocent flower, / But be the serpent under't'. Some critics believe that a line in Act 2 Scene 3 ('dire combustion and confused events') refers to the gunpowder plot.

There are, of course, many other examples of Shakespeare's use of contemporary knowledge and events in *Macbeth*. What follows identifies significant social and cultural contexts of the time that influenced the creation of *Macbeth*: witchcraft, attitudes to women, prophecy, succession and divine right.

Witchcraft

When *Macbeth* was written, witchcraft was controversial, chiefly because of King James's great interest in the issue. As noted above, James published his *Demonologie* in 1597, prompted by disturbing experiences during a visit to Denmark in 1589. He had gone there to bring his new queen, Anne, back to Scotland, but was delayed by storms, which he believed were stirred up by witches. While in Denmark, he read the theories of continental experts about covens, compacts with the devil and secret marks on the bodies of those who had had contact with witches. He came to believe that witches might be conspiring against the very person of the king. Witchcraft thus became associated with treason, and James began a witch-hunt in Scotland that lasted for most of the 1590s.

One famous trial was that of the North Berwick witches. They were led by Agnes Sampson and a sorcerer/schoolmaster, Doctor Fian. The pamphlet *News from Scotland* reports that Sampson was able to repeat private conversations held between King James and his queen on their wedding night. It also claimed that Sampson was preparing toad venom to poison the king. The pamphlet described their contracts with the devil:

> and forasmuch as by due examination of witchcraft and witches in Scotland, it hath lately been found that the Devil doth generally mark them with a privy mark, by reason the witches have confessed themselves, that the Devil doth lick them with his tongue in some privy part of their body, before he doth receive them to be his servants.

Shakespeare perhaps alludes to this 'contract' when Lady Macbeth rubs at the 'damned spot' of Duncan's blood, which cannot be removed. Earlier, like a witch, she had called on the dark powers to possess her and remove her femininity. For Jacobeans therefore, Macbeth was in contact with strange, deviant womanhood at home as well as on the heath.

In Shakespeare's time, belief in witchcraft had authority from the Bible, notably the story of the Witch of Endor. Such stories and prohibitions had encouraged witch-hunts and terrible tortures of victims for centuries throughout western Europe. In many periods of history Christians persecuted what they saw as deviant behaviour, believing the existence of witches identified an evil that must be eliminated. Zealots (usually male) pursued outcasts (usually women) and declared them to be witches. In *Demonologie*, James declared that evil practices were committed by 20 women for every one man.

Witches were often thought to have power over sexual performance. King James wrote that Satan was the primary lover for witches and that 'the devil squeezed generative fluid from the sexual organs of dead men for potency with the women who served him'. Productions that demonise Lady Macbeth often suggest that she has a mysterious, devil-inspired control over her husband's sexuality. Other interpretations use the Witch's line 'I'll do, I'll do, and I'll do' in Act 1 Scene 3 to suggest that her sexual assault on the sailor (or Macbeth) will drain him of potency.

When James came to London as king in 1603 he met more varied responses to witchcraft than he had found in Scotland. Nonetheless, the English were fascinated by the occult: witches were thought to fly, sail in a sieve, and bring darkness, fogs and storms. Each worked through her 'familiar' – an animal, reptile or bird (the 'Graymalkin' and 'Paddock' of the opening scene). Shakespeare uses such beliefs in his Witches' language and practices. He showed the effects on the man who is tempted by them, made even more powerful by the fact that he was a great military hero:

- Macbeth becomes 'rapt' in a trance.
- He sees visions.
- He is unable to pray.
- At first, he is normal in suffering from fear, but eventually he claims 'I have almost forgot the taste of fears'.

In 1604 Parliament passed a statute strengthening laws against witchcraft. However, perhaps responding privately to sceptical views, James himself seems to have relaxed his own intense persecution of witches. He took an interest in certain trials, advised more circumspect attitudes and in particular doubted the accusations made by children.

In *Macbeth* Banquo refers to the Witches' ugliness: Banquo describes them as bearded and withered. In the Folio of 1623 they describe themselves as 'the weyward sisters' (Act 1 Scene 3), which later editors have amended to 'weïrd' (from 'wyrd', meaning 'destiny'). 'Weyward' suggests alternative, eccentric, perhaps disruptive, but not necessarily foul and ugly. They are sometimes played onstage less as witches than as Fates, supervisors rather than determiners of destiny (in Anglo-Saxon 'weird' approximately means 'fate').

Audiences in Shakespeare's playhouse would hold a very wide range of attitudes towards the Witches. Some would see them as an embodiment of evil, others would merely accept that assumption for the purposes of the play, suspending their scepticism about witchcraft for the period of the performance.

Shakespeare himself may have had doubts about how far he wanted the Witches to represent evil. The play suggests that his imagination was far more deeply stirred by the dark solitude of Macbeth's mind than by the external appearance and procedures of the Witches.

Women

As the preceding discussion of witchcraft shows, Shakespeare's England treated women as inferiors. King James's researches into witchcraft were influenced by the *Malleus Malleficarum* (*The Hammer of Witches*) written in 1486. This was a strikingly misogynistic work, implying that women are inherently more susceptible to evil than men, as shown when Satan, disguised as a serpent, first tempted Eve, who then tempted Adam. Shakespeare recalls this original sin when Lady Macbeth uses her sexual power over her husband, and persuades him to evil. She uses the image of a serpent hiding beneath a flower to encourage him into a performance of deceitful welcome which will disarm Duncan. Such hypocrisy was more associated with the woman than the man.

Such beliefs were commonly accepted in the patriarchal society that was Elizabethan and Jacobean England. Women had few rights and were expected to be obedient first to their father and then to their husband. Their proper sphere was the home, whilst men worked, travelled, engaged in society and politics and made the major decisions that affected the family.

In dramatising the story of Macbeth in eleventh-century Scotland, Shakespeare depicts a warlike culture that is even more male-dominated, like the Old English epic poem *Beowulf*, which suggests that the role of women was to emphasise their separateness and to minister as hostesses to the men. Macbeth's Scotland derives from that Anglo-Saxon society. Shakespeare presents Lady Macbeth fulfilling her role graciously with Duncan when he arrives at the castle, and in the banquet of Act 3 she attempts the duties of a queen but is eventually unable to sustain the pretence.

However, Lady Macbeth defies such conventional and submissive female stereotyping. Her independence and strength of purpose was uncommon on the Elizabethan stage, even though Jacobean plays included women who asserted themselves at the expense of men, taking men's roles and assuming some masculine qualities. Shakespeare's Cleopatra, Webster's Duchess of Malfi and Vittoria Corombona (in *The White Devil*) are examples of female characters who combine stern resolve with feminine sexuality.

Lady Macbeth's sexuality is strange and paradoxical. She clearly has a strong hold over her husband. But just before his arrival in Act 1 Scene 5, she urges the powers of darkness to remove her womanly nature:

> make thick my blood,
> Stop up th'access and passage to remorse
> That no compunctious visitings of nature
> Shake my fell purpose   *(Act 1 Scene 5, lines 41–4)*

She wishes her blood to become abnormal, and that her monthly menstrual flow may stop. The passage to the womb was equated with the passage to the womanly feelings of tenderness. She also demands that her milk be turned to gall. Her appeal denies the two womanly instincts of giving birth and of suckling her child.

'Milk' and 'blood' convey strong meanings throughout the play, in particular the distinction between the female and the male. Lady Macbeth deplores 'the milk of human kindness' in Macbeth. Although he is used to blood on the battlefield, she feels he has too much of the feminine in him to shed Duncan's blood in the bedchamber. She orders the spirits to possess her with masculine qualities in order to compensate for his weakness. He seems awed by her intensity: 'Bring forth men-children only'.

Prophecy

Prophecy is a powerful force in the play. In Act 1 the Witches accost Macbeth on his 'day of success' and they promise him an even more impressive future. In the first two acts their greetings are fulfilled as he becomes Thane of Cawdor and then king of Scotland, but the achievement brings no comfort to Macbeth. In Act 4 it is he who takes the initiative: he visits them and demands more insights into his future. This time the prophecies are more ambiguous and they mingle reassurance with warnings.

Both Macbeth and Banquo are ambivalent in their attitudes to prophecy. They are eager to know what is usually kept hidden, but they also feel alarmed. Even when Macbeth is given his first, legitimate, reward and becomes Thane of Cawdor, Banquo's instinctive reaction is 'What, can the devil speak true?' Their uncertainty and apprehension reflect contemporary attitudes. Prophecy could be regarded as an act of treason in Elizabethan and Jacobean England. Any uprising could gain a dangerous authority if it was thought to be predicted and therefore ordained. Its leader could present himself not as an upstart but as being obedient to destiny.

However, prophecy could also be used by the political establishment to provide helpful public relations. After the years of anxiety about who would succeed Elizabeth, James's position was not wholly secure. He claimed that his Stuart family was descended from Banquo, whose descendants the Witches had prophesied would be kings. Shakespeare, perhaps writing partly to please the king, reinforces this claim with his story of Fleance's escape in Act 3. The tyrant Macbeth is troubled by 'the seed of Banquo' inheriting the throne and is shaken when the Murderer tells him that they failed to kill Fleance. When he sees the vision of the line of kings he is appalled by the sense of its lasting glory beyond the brief span of his own life. King James's claim to be descended from Banquo is thus given extra moral force in the play because the prophecy to Banquo not only threatens the play's ruthless tyrant but guarantees James's legitimacy.

In 1605, only a few months before Shakespeare wrote *Macbeth*, the king visited Oxford and was welcomed with an entertainment titled *Tres Sibyllae* (*Three Sibylls*) in which counterparts of the three 'weïrd sisters' congratulated him on his ancestry, celebrating the fact that the prophecy made to Banquo was now fulfilled and prophesying further success for James and his descendants. Such supernatural support seemed appropriate to a monarch like James, whose letters to his son (see page 79) asserted the divine right of kings. Since many Old Testament prophecies were fulfilled in the birth of Christ, why should not later prophecies be fulfilled in the triumphs of a Christian king, who has been anointed by God?

The most perplexing question about prophecy in *Macbeth* is connected with the hero/criminal's free will. Does he choose to murder? Or do the prophecies ensure that his actions are predestined and that he has no choice but to murder Duncan? It may be that the

Witches know before they meet Macbeth what he will decide to do, that they reinforce the temptation in his mind and that this constitutes a pressure towards the act of murder. But he still has the choice to refrain from evil. He acknowledges that he could simply wait for the future to unfold:

> If chance will have me king, why chance may crown me
> Without my stir.   *(Act 1 Scene 3, lines 142–3)*

Banquo is also tempted, but he behaves differently. His refusal to act may be interpreted as a virtuous submission to the way events will inevitably work themselves out. In this respect, Shakespeare makes him an important contrast to Macbeth, since both are successful generals, both hear what the Witches prophesy and both are troubled by the dangers of being tempted. However, some critics see Banquo as a coward or, at the least, morally flawed, because he suspects that Macbeth has tried to interfere with fate. At the end of Act 2 he could have used his knowledge of the prophecies and acted on his suspicions of Macbeth, but he chooses not to expose the crime.

On hearing the prophecies, Macbeth can choose to remain within the virtuous hierarchy of Duncan's court or he can choose the evil course that will lead to a desolate solitude. It is true that the Witches present him with a tempting picture of himself as king at some time in his future, that this temptation constitutes a type of pressure, and that Lady Macbeth then tempts him in a more intimate way. But the temptations and their pressures do not deprive him of free will. He knowingly chooses the way of damnation.

The succession to the throne

Shakespeare's contemporaries believed in primogeniture – that the eldest son (or, failing that, daughter) should inherit the father's title. However, the issue of succession to the throne became increasingly controversial in Queen Elizabeth's reign, and in 1572 the Second Treasons Act forbade any debate about it. Nonetheless, in the 1590s, with the queen ageing and childless, there was widespread concern about who would succeed her. James was the son of her Catholic enemy, Mary, Queen of Scots, and although he could claim legitimate right to the throne deriving from Henry VII, this did not silence controversy, which revolved around three crucial questions:

- On what grounds should the crown pass from one king to another?
- Should Parliament and the people have a voice in the succession?
- Is it ever right to depose a monarch?

Religious disputes complicated the issue. Some Catholics supported James's claim to the English throne, believing that, though he was avowedly a Protestant, he would bring his mother's Catholicism to England.

In *Macbeth* the issue of succession is complicated, but the same three questions still have telling urgency. The established Scottish principle was tanistry (election from a small group of kinsmen). This often led to assassination when a potential successor to the throne chose a favourable moment to make himself prominent. Historically, Macbeth had a good claim to the crown, and Holinshed records that Macbeth's thoughts of killing Duncan became serious only when Duncan provocatively broke with tradition by appointing Malcolm as Prince of Cumberland. By tradition Malcolm had no more right to the throne than Macbeth, who (if there were to be an election) would have the advantage of being a successful military leader at a time of great crisis.

Shakespeare does not follow Holinshed in criticising Duncan for appointing Malcolm as his heir. By altering his source material in this respect, Shakespeare makes Macbeth a usurper before he becomes a tyrant. Shakespeare is vague about how Macbeth gains the throne, but a consideration of how characters react to the crisis of Duncan's death is suggestive:

- When Duncan's murder is discovered, Banquo takes the lead in trying to calm the distress and confusion. He speaks of fighting against 'treasonous malice' and of an immediate meeting. There is no word of the succession.
- Malcolm, as Prince of Cumberland, might be expected to assert himself. But he feels confused and vulnerable. His flight makes it easier for the Scottish nobles to revert to the principle of election and to choose the strongest leader as king.
- Scotland's choice of Macbeth (or perhaps his simply taking the throne) happens offstage. Ross speaks of it imprecisely:

Then 'tis most like
The sovereignty will fall upon Macbeth.

(Act 2 Scene 4, lines 29–30)

- Macduff answers that 'He is already named and gone to Scone / To be invested.' Macduff is clearly worried by either the principle or the speed of Macbeth's promotion.
- Banquo expresses a similar concern ten lines later: 'Thou hast it now . . .'. He too does not elaborate on Macbeth's methods, but expresses his generalised concern: 'I fear / Thou played'st most foully for't.'

After the start of Act 3, no one mentions the Scottish principle of electing the king. Most characters seem to assume primogeniture:
- Macbeth fears that the sceptre will be 'wrenched' from him, 'no son of mine succeeding'.
- The Witches show an unbroken tradition of male heirs established by Banquo.
- In England Malcolm appears to see himself as his father's heir.
- Macduff comes to England to persuade Malcolm to return as king. He says nothing about Malcolm's having to be elected. When persuaded of Malcolm's 'wickedness' he declares that his hopes have ended, therefore implying that there is no alternative king.
- In his final speech Macduff hails Malcolm as king: 'for so thou art'. He gives no sign that an election is necessary.

Whilst some critics believe that King James would be unlikely to welcome *Macbeth*, with its unresolved issue of heredity or election to the throne, that view may well be mistaken. After all, James watched the play, would almost certainly have approved its apparent endorsement of his right to rule as a supposed descendant of Banquo, and would have approved of the tyrant Macbeth being overthrown by the son of the murdered King Duncan. James's anxieties about succession were evident. He felt in danger of being deposed while he was king of Scotland, and soon after becoming king in England he faced the alarming dangers of the gunpowder plot in 1605. His own mother and father had met violent deaths and King James continually wore padded garments as a protection against assassins.

But King James was confident in his belief in primogeniture, rather than the ancient Scottish tradition of election. He wrote:

> Monarchy is the true pattern of divinity . . . the lineal
> succession of crowns being begun among the people of God

. . . at the very moment of the expiring of the king reigning, the nearest and lawful heir entereth in his place.

The divine right of kings

Queen Elizabeth wrote little about her monarchical beliefs, so perpetuating the sense of mystery that was part of her status as Virgin Queen. However, James wrote a good deal on the monarchy. *The True Law of Free Monarchies* and *Basilikon Doron* (written as advice to his son, Prince Henry) were both published before he became king of England. They were reprinted and much read in London from 1603.

James believed in the absolute powers of the monarch. His view was that a king's position derives from God and not from the people's consent, therefore only God has the power to depose a king. James referred to the biblical King Saul, who was notably corrupt: 'we never read that ever the prophets persuaded the people to rebel against the prince, however wicked soever he was'. Even a tyrannical king must be accepted by the people, who must trust that God in His good time may remove him. In practice, James softened these views, advising his son that it is more prudent to act with consent.

Act 4 Scene 3 of *Macbeth* raises the question of whether or not it is justified to remove a bad king. Malcolm and Macduff are wary of each other but they agree that Macbeth must be removed, and by human beings, with the presumed support of God. Malcolm does not consider taking personal revenge, nor does he mention the murder of his father. He agrees with Macduff that it is Scotland that suffers under Macbeth's regime, and so the tyrant king must be removed for the sake of the people. Malcolm and Macduff barely mention the fact that Macbeth usurped the throne. They refer to Macbeth as 'the tyrant' and from this point the word is often used instead of his name.

Holinshed wrote of Macbeth ruling well for ten years, but Shakespeare ignores this, so strengthening the view of Macbeth as tyranny personified. Unlike King James, Shakespeare appears to accept that a tyrant king may be deposed by his suffering subjects: Macbeth is defeated by popular resistance led by a foreign invasion. Some critics have found it ironic that King James felt he owed his position as king (through the myth of Banquo and the Stuart line) to Malcolm and Macduff's rebellion, an act that defies James's belief in a king's divine right to rule.

Language

The language of the play is taut and dense, matching its rapid action and the intense emotions of the main characters. It presents the hero's nightmare struggles, his doubts and decisions in language full of ambiguity and uncertainty. There are many questions and unresolved antitheses: 'Not so happy, yet much happier'; 'This supernatural soliciting / Cannot be ill, cannot be good'; 'Good sir, why do you start and seem to fear / Things that do sound so fair?'

Certain words and phrases recur creating a sense of foreboding: 'blood', 'darkness', 'man', 'done', 'time'. These words help to create what the critic Wilson Knight called 'The Metaphysic of Evil' and Wilbur Sanders called 'An Unknown Fear'. Both phrases are titles of chapters in their writings which explore how the language of the play contributes to the sense of uncertainty.

Ben Jonson famously remarked that Shakespeare 'wanted art' (lacked technical skill). But that comment is mistaken, as is the notion of Shakespeare as a 'natural' writer, utterly spontaneous, inspired only by his incandescent imagination. Even in a play like *Macbeth*, which delves so deeply into the main character's uniquely individual imagination, Shakespeare was using and developing rhetorical skills of his own and previous times. What follows are some of the language techniques he uses in *Macbeth* to intensify dramatic effect and to create mood and character.

Imagery
Macbeth is rich in imagery: vivid words and phrases that conjure up emotionally-charged pictures in the imagination:

> Where our fate hid in an auger hole may rush / And seize us
> *(Act 2 Scene 3, line 115)*

> The cistern of my lust   *(Act 4 Scene 3, line 63)*

> Raze out the written troubles of the brain
> *(Act 5 Scene 3, line 43)*

All Shakespeare's imagery uses metaphor, simile or personification. All of these are comparisons. A simile compares one thing to another using 'like' or 'as' (Malcolm suggests that Macbeth will seem 'as pure as snow'; Duncan rewards his subjects with signs of nobleness 'like stars'). A metaphor is usually more compact, suggesting that two dissimilar things are actually the same. Macduff, describing the holy self-denial of Malcolm's mother, declares that she 'Died every day she lived'. Personification turns inanimate things into persons, giving them human feelings or attributes, as when the Captain sees 'Fortune' smiling on the rebel Macdonald, and Macbeth as 'Valour's minion'.

In all Shakespeare's plays, images do not just make vivid the moment or thing they describe. They give pleasure as they stir the audience's imagination, deepen dramatic impact, and provide insight into character. Certain images are often repeated in varied ways and run through the play.

Blood

The play begins and ends with bloodshed in battle, and horrific murders dominate much of the action in between. Images of blood carry great emotional force and intensify meaning: 'Make thick my blood'; 'the fountain of your blood'; 'badged with blood'; 'the nea'er in blood, / The nearer bloody'; 'the blood-boltered Banquo'. Macbeth looks at his 'hangman's hands' (his image is of the hangman's job to disembowel the criminal). Macbeth describes Duncan's blood not with its literal red colour but metaphorically, to assert the significance of the loss: 'His silver skin laced with his golden blood'. After the banquet he realises that he can never escape the bloody consequences of his actions:

It will have blood they say: blood will have blood.

(Act 3 Scene 4, line 122)

His obsession leads him into the hyperbole of wading through a river of blood, so that going on or turning back are equally 'tedious'. Lady Macbeth smells blood and rubs obsessively at an imagined spot on her hands. The blood of the invading army will act like 'dew' on a flower and 'drown the weeds'.

Darkness

Many of the scenes occur at night and the frequent images of darkness help create the sense of evil that pervades much of the play:

> Let not light see my black and deep desires
>
> *(Act 1 Scene 4, line 51)*

> dark night strangles the travelling lamp   *(Act 2 Scene 4, line 7)*

> Come seeling night, / Scarf up the tender eye of pitiful day
>
> *(Act 3 Scene 2, lines 46–7)*

> Life's but a walking shadow   *(Act 5 Scene 5, line 23)*

Nature

Nature can be benign and productive. Duncan has 'begun to plant' Macbeth and will labour to make him 'full of growing'. Banquo speaks of returning a potential 'harvest' to his king. In the play's last speech, Malcolm says that there is much to do, which 'would be planted newly with the time'. There are many references to creatures. Banquo and Duncan value the birds that seem to bring gentleness and peace to the battlements of Macbeth's castle. Lady Macduff speaks of the 'poor wren' which fights courageously to defend her loved ones against the owl.

Nature can also threaten, as shown through images of creatures which represent ferocity. When faced with the unreal mockery of the Ghost, Macbeth would prefer to confront a bear, rhinoceros or tiger. Macduff compares a lustful man to a 'vulture'. Macbeth, in his dagger soliloquy, thinks of the wolf as the appropriate sentinel for the personified 'withered murder'. Macbeth's mind is 'full of scorpions' and he is wary of the snake (Fleance) which he has 'scotch'd', not killed.

Shakespeare shows how evil takes over Scotland by using images of nature disturbed and reversed. When Macbeth asks the Witches to 'look into the seeds of time', he is using (in 'seeds') one of the play's benign images, but visiting the Witches in Act 4 he imagines 'germen' (seeds) tumbling to chaos. Duncan's murder is 'a breach in nature / For ruin's wasteful entrance'. It is claimed that his horses ate each other and

A falcon tow'ring in her pride of place
Was by a mousing owl hawked at and killed.

(Act 2 Scene 4, lines 12–13)

Disease

The Witches' 'fog and filthy air' in the first scene begins the imagery of disease. The First Witch will make the sailor 'dwindle, peak, and pine', and she puts 'poisoned entrails' and 'Sweltered venom' in the cauldron. When the Witches disappear, Macbeth curses them: 'Infected be the air whereon they ride.'

Much of the sickness infects the mind. The Doctor judges that Lady Macbeth's sickness is more spiritual and psychological than physical. Macbeth often describes his own mental state: 'my seated heart knock at my ribs'; 'the heat-oppressed brain', and his confession to the murderers about Banquo that (we) 'wear our health but sickly in his life'.

In Act 5 Caithness describes Malcolm as 'the med'cine of the sickly weal'. The blood the invaders prepare to shed will purge away the sickness. The play's most obvious healer is Edward the Confessor of England. He never appears, but is said to possess a special gift of curing 'strangely visited people'. His 'healing benediction' is supported by heavenly 'grace', and he passes the gift to his descendants.

Clothes

Shakespeare uses the image of clothes to show a feeling of discomfort, unfamiliarity or inappropriateness. Banquo comments to Ross about why Macbeth has become introspective on becoming Thane of Cawdor:

New honours come upon him
Like our strange garments   *(Act 1 Scene 3, lines 143–4)*

Macbeth feels he must get used to the new honours Duncan has given him. They should 'be worn now in their newest gloss, / Not cast aside so soon', but as Malcolm's army moves closer to Dunsinane, Caithness describes Macbeth's inability to impose good order:

He cannot buckle his distempered cause
Within the belt of rule.   *(Act 5 Scene 2, lines 15–16)*

Angus sees Macbeth as a shrunken leader, and his image of clothing mocks the wearer, describing the absurdity:

> Now does he feel his title
> Hang loose about him, like a giant's robe
> Upon a dwarfish thief.   *(Act 5 Scene 2, lines 20–2)*

Macbeth was never particularly skilful at playing the hypocrite. Angus describes the absurdity of the thief pretending to be a giant. Macbeth is like a player pretending to be king.

A modern production made concrete the image of clothing by having the king's magnificent jewelled robe onstage throughout, so giving the impression that the office of king was always distinct from the man who temporarily occupied it.

Time

Time is both a source of imagery and a philosophical issue. Characters regard time in various ways:

- Time present: Lady Macbeth refers to contemporary people, their behaviour, concerns and judgements when she instructs her husband in hypocrisy: 'To beguile the time, / Look like the time.'
- The passage of time: normal time is marked by the distinctiveness of light versus darkness, of day versus night, a uniqueness which Macbeth and his wife try to blur: 'Come thick night . . .', 'Stars, hide your fires . . .'. After the banquet Lady Macbeth speaks of night 'Almost at odds with morning', so implying that time is at war with itself.
- Time personified: Macbeth, hearing that Macduff has escaped him, personifies time as a power that cannot be tricked or defeated: 'Time, thou anticipat'st my dread exploits.'
- Time's value: when he hears of his wife's death, Macbeth regrets that there is now not a 'time' to respond appropriately. Time is reduced to a 'petty pace', a mere succession of meaningless moments.
- The intensity of a particular moment in time: Lady Macbeth, excited by her husband's letter and his arrival, dismisses 'this ignorant present' and declares, 'I feel now / The future in the instant.'
- Time as linking cause and effect: moments of time cannot stand alone: they are connected to the past and the future. However,

Macbeth wishes that the single act of murdering Duncan might have no consequences:

> that but this blow
> Might be the be-all and the end-all – here,
> But here, upon this bank and shoal of time,
> We'd jump the life to come.　　　　*(Act 1 Scene 7, lines 4–7)*

Antithesis

Antithesis is the opposition of ideas, words or phrases against each other, and gives force to many plays, since conflict is the essence of drama. Antithesis is especially powerful in *Macbeth*, where character is set against character, and equivocation, or double-speaking, is a major theme. The Witches often speak antithetically: 'When the battle's lost, and won'; 'Lesser than Macbeth, and greater'; 'Hear his speech, but say thou nought.' Their chorused, compact antithesis, 'Fair is foul, and foul is fair' is one of the play's dominant motifs.

In Act 5 Macbeth comes to realise how the Witches have been deceiving him when he speaks of 'the equivocation of the fiend / That lies like truth'. Lies and truth are opposite in meaning, but are made similar in the word 'like'. His comment is both antithesis and paradox. Soon afterwards he gives an angry summary of how he has been tricked in declaring that they 'keep the word of promise to our ear / And break it to our hope'.

When the murder has brought status but not security, Macbeth makes a sardonic comment on his situation:

> Better be with the dead
> Whom we, to gain our peace, have sent to peace
> 　　　　　　　　　　*(Act 3 Scene 2, lines 19–20)*

'Peace' has the two ironically opposite meanings of comfort and death. A further antithesis is in 'gain', implying that something comes towards the speaker, as opposed to 'sent'.

Antithesis may help a character to redefine what used to be familiar. Ross tells Macduff that Scotland 'cannot / Be called our mother, but our grave'. He feels he must stop thinking of his 'mother' country and lose the comforting notion of the place that gave him birth and life.

Sometimes antithesis is descriptive. For example, when Macbeth evokes a new world of evil the transition from good is strengthened not only by the oppositions of 'good things' with 'black agents' and day versus night, but also by the opposite meanings of the rhyming words:

> Good things of day begin to droop and drowse,
> Whiles night's black agents to their preys do rouse.
>
> *(Act 3 Scene 2, lines 52–3)*

'Begin to droop and drowse' describes the gradual decline of goodness, whereas the sharper single verb 'do rouse' suggests an energetic predator.

Soliloquy

Through soliloquy, Shakespeare enables the audience to gain direct experience of a character's mind. A soliloquy is a kind of internal debate spoken by a character who is alone onstage, or believes himself to be alone. In this play Macbeth's asides can also be seen as soliloquies. It is a dramatic convention that a soliloquy reveals a character's true thoughts and feelings.

Most of the soliloquies are spoken by Macbeth and all show him exploring his state of mind: fear, guilt, confusion, uncertainty and despair. He chooses the path to self-destruction and he experiences damnation whilst still alive. The language which explores this state of mind contains troubling vagueness, such as 'nothing is, / But what is not' where the seemingly precise antithesis barely conceals infinite ambiguity.

Sometimes a soliloquy is a reaction to a terrifying moment, as in Act 2 when Macbeth thinks he sees the dagger leading him to murder. Elsewhere, as in Act 3 Scene 1, it explores a particular frustration – the inhibiting presence of Banquo. In Act 5 the 'Tomorrow' soliloquy expresses Macbeth's overwhelming despair. Lady Macbeth's first scene contains one of the play's most intense soliloquies. She calls passionately on demonic spirits to possess her and to create a world committed to evil. You can find discussion of particular soliloquies on pages 9, 12, 15, 18 and 55.

Lists

Shakespeare often accumulates words and phrases rather like a list. One of the most grotesque examples occurs in the Witches' major scene, as part of their preparation for Macbeth. The fragments of body parts, so precisely listed, are placed in the cauldron, as though from an infernal recipe. Listing can be turned to a more comic effect, as when the Porter uses a list of antitheses on drink to show how alcohol disables sexual performance. Shakespeare is using alcohol as a metaphor for equivocation, and each item increases the importance of equivocation as a motif in the play and helps to show its subversive qualities:

> it makes him, and it mars him; it sets him on, and it takes him off; it persuades him and disheartens him, makes him stand to and not stand to. *(Act 2 Scene 3, lines 26–8)*

When Macbeth lists types of dogs in his instructions to the murderers in Act 3 Scene 1, it becomes a sustained sneer at the expense of different types of men and helps to bully the murderers into compliance. Sometimes a list conveys obsession, as with Macbeth's descriptions of sleep immediately after the murder or when he complains at the impotence of violence against a dead man:

> nor steel nor poison,
> Malice domestic, foreign levy, nothing
> Can touch him further. *(Act 3 Scene 2, lines 24–6)*

Malcolm has a conscious rhetorical purpose when he uses lists to deceive and test Macduff. He catalogues Macbeth's vices ('bloody, / Luxurious, avaricious . . .') and then gives two lists of examples of his own sexual appetite and avarice that run through the next two speeches dedicated to blackening his own name. When Macduff appears to tolerate such listed vices, Malcolm turns to a twelve-item list of positives in order to negate them:

> The king-becoming graces –
> As justice, verity, temp'rance, stableness,
> Bounty, perseverance, mercy, lowliness,
> Devotion, patience, courage, fortitude –
> I have no relish of them *(Act 4 Scene 3, lines 91–5)*

The contrast with Macbeth is evident, and Malcolm's persuasive intention in doing this becomes clear soon afterwards, but the dramatic effect of this list is to detach the virtues of kingship from any particular king. The context makes them sound like strange abstractions distanced from immediate experience.

Repetition

Repetition of a word or a phrase can give great emotional force to a moment (see page 80). *Macbeth* explores the nature and practices of evil, which include parodies of religious ritual. When she invokes 'the murd'ring ministers' in Act 1 Scene 5, Lady Macbeth heightens her language by repeating imperatives: 'Come, you spirits'; 'Come to my woman's breasts'; 'Come, thick night'. When Macbeth visits the Witches for more information, he begins with a formal 'I conjure you . . .' and continues his rhetoric by repeating 'though' to introduce each example of disorder: 'Though you untie . . .'; 'though the yeasty waves . . .'; 'Though bladed corn . . .'; 'Though castles . . .'.

The Witches greet Macbeth in Act 1 Scene 3 with three formal 'All hail's, then address Banquo more simply with three 'Hail's, followed by the three paradoxes that compare him with Macbeth. They repeat the sequence of three in the more detailed prophecies in Act 4. When privately conducting their ceremonies, they chorus the lines, in which, as with most ritual language, whether for good or evil, repetition works strongly in assonance, alliteration and rhyme:

> Double, double toil and trouble;
> Fire burn, and cauldron bubble.   *(Act 4 Scene 1, lines 10–11)*

Rhyme is used in tetrameters (lines with a four-beat rhythm) for incantatory effects in the Witches' scenes and helps to convey the weird ambivalence of horror and absurdity in their language. As in all Shakespeare's plays, rhyme helps to close a scene or episode. Sometimes the effect is ironic and ominous, as in the four rhyming words at the end of Act 1 Scene 2: 'death', 'Macbeth', 'done', 'won'. After submitting to his wife's pressure, Macbeth deeply regrets what he is about to do, as his rhyming words emphasise the difference between the surface behaviour ('show') and true awareness ('know'):

> Away, and mock the time with fairest show,
> False face must hide what the false heart doth know.

(Act 1 Scene 7, lines 81–2)

Verse and prose

Shakespeare's audiences expected tragedies to be written in verse. The heightened poetic style was thought to be particularly suitable for kings, great affairs of state, tragic themes and moments of dramatic or emotional intensity. Much of the language in *Macbeth* is blank verse: unrhymed verse written in iambic pentameter. It is conventional to define iambic pentameter as a rhythm or metre in which each line has five stressed syllables (/) alternating with five unstressed syllables (×):

> × / × / × / × / × /
> And purge it to a sound and pristine health

At school Shakespeare had learned the technical definition of iambic pentameter. In Latin *penta* means five, and *iamb* means a 'foot' of two syllables, the first unstressed, the second stressed (as in 'Macbeth': MacBETH). In his early plays much of the metre is regular, with most lines 'end-stopped' (each line making sense on its own, usually supported by decisive punctuation).

By the time Shakespeare wrote *Macbeth*, end-stopping is less frequent. There is greater use of enjambment (running on) where one line flows on to the next, seemingly with little or no pause:

> Thriftless ambition that will ravin up
> Thine own life's means. Then 'tis most like
> The sovereignty will fall upon Macbeth.

(Act 2 Scene 4, lines 28–30)

> Augures, and understood relations, have
> By maggot-pies, and choughs, and rooks brought forth
> The secret'st man of blood.

(Act 3 Scene 4, lines 124–6)

The 'five-beat' rhythm is less obviously prominent, though usually still present. Lines can have more or fewer than ten syllables. Actors can use their discretion in how to deliver the lines; they can pause or emphasise to avoid mechanical-sounding delivery of the iambic pentameter. So it is appropriate when studying or acting in *Macbeth* not to apply a rigid rule about how the verse should be spoken. Shakespeare used the convention of the iambic pentameter, but he did not adhere to it slavishly. He was prepared to break the rules to suit his dramatic purpose.

The Witches use tetrameter metre which helps to isolate them from the 'normal' world, and their often childlike rhythms give a playful and often mocking quality to their words. Tetrameters, with their strong, often hypnotic beat, also contribute to the Witches' rituals:

> The weïrd sisters, hand in hand,
> Posters of the sea and land,
> Thus do go, about, about,
> Thrice to thine, and thrice to mine,
> And thrice again, to make up nine.   *(Act 1 Scene 3, lines 30–4)*

Less than ten per cent of the play is in prose. One of Shakespeare's reasons for occasionally using prose is that he followed theatrical convention: prose was felt to be appropriate for:

- low-status characters, such as the Porter;
- characters in a state of madness, as in Lady Macbeth's sleep-walking;
- letters, as when Lady Macbeth reads about the Witches;
- comedy, with the Porter and Lady Macduff and her son.

Shakespeare sometimes switches between verse and prose within a single episode, as with Macbeth's discussion with the Murderers and Lady Macduff's talk with her son. These changes mark a change in mood or fulfil a dramatic function. Elizabethan and Jacobean audiences went to the theatre to 'hear' a play, and were alert to the changed rhythms and significances of switches from verse to prose.

Critical approaches

Traditional criticism

The best known eighteenth-century critic, Dr Samuel Johnson, responded ambivalently to *Macbeth*:

> This play is deservedly celebrated for the propriety of its fictions, and solemnity, grandeur, and variety of its action; but it has no nice discriminations of character, the events are too great to admit the influence of particular dispositions, and the course of the action necessarily determines the conduct of the agents.

Johnson finds limited interest in Shakespeare's characterisation; for example, he declares that Lady Macbeth is 'merely detested'. Johnson was one of the first critics to analyse Shakespeare's language, the imagery in particular, and he objects to the impropriety of Lady Macbeth's wordplay on 'gild' and 'gilt' in Act 2. Johnson approves of the play's warning about the dangers of ambition; like some earlier critics, he praises Shakespeare's intuition, which expresses tendencies and passions that are universal in human nature. However, he also feels that Shakespeare is a victim of his credulous times, when people were all too ready to believe. He claims that in creating the Witches Shakespeare was responding to King James's interest in the occult, and that the scenes of the supernatural are likely to be ridiculed by audiences and readers in Johnson's own rationalist century.

However, in the second half of the eighteenth century and throughout the nineteenth, approval of Shakespeare came close to worship. He was hailed as 'the poet of nature', almost a god in his creativity. One of the most celebrated essays on *Macbeth*, by Thomas de Quincey in 1823, ends with a burst of praise:

> O mighty poet! Thy works are not as those of men, simply and merely great works of art; but are also like the phenomena of nature.

De Quincey's essay, 'On the Knocking on the Gate in *Macbeth*', like much Romantic criticism, is highly personal. He wonders why this moment from Act 2 affects his feelings so strongly, when his objective understanding is less impressed. His explanation depends strongly on identification with character – but with the murderers rather than with Duncan, the victim. Both Macbeth and his wife 'are conformed to the image of devils' and exist, as it were, in another world, 'locked up and sequestered in some deep recess'. When they hear the knocking on the gate, 'the pulses of life are beginning to beat again' and they and the audience have to re-enter the normal world after the nightmare of the murder. De Quincey's essay, though short, has been much praised for its psychological insights.

The Romantic poet/philosopher Coleridge lectured on *Macbeth* in 1813. He greatly admired 'the Weird Sisters as the key-note of the character of the whole play' and opposed the 'vulgar stage error' which diminished them into witches with broomsticks. Unlike Dr Johnson, Coleridge was fascinated by Lady Macbeth's womanliness trying to cultivate devilish insensitivity and by the combined power and subtlety of the language in Act 1, which describes Macbeth being tempted. However, Coleridge could not accept the sudden incongruity of the Porter's appearance:

> This low Porter soliloquy I believe written for the mob by
> some other hand, perhaps with Shakespeare's consent – and
> that, finding it take, he with the remaining ink of a pen
> otherwise employed just interpolated it with the sentence 'I'll
> devil-porter it no further' and what follows to 'bonfire'.

Coleridge is typical of many traditional critics in responding to the nightmare world of *Macbeth*, to the ways in which the pace of the action and the power of language create a sense of the hero's imagination. Jonathan Bate, in *The Genius of Shakespeare* (1997), analyses the paintings of the Romantic artist Henry Fuseli, who was especially fascinated by Macbeth and the horror of his life as 'a walking shadow'. Fuseli's various paintings of the Witches in *Macbeth* are well-known images. Bate summarises his own response to Fuseli's response to Shakespeare:

> When the Romantic . . . looks at Macbeth, he does not only see
> an icon of humankind's capacity to make a contract with evil:
> he sees his own highest imaginings, in all their thrilling power,
> in all their darkness.

Many traditional critics identify with characters in the play about which they write. Shakespeare is often praised for the 'universality' of his characters: their thoughts and passions can be felt by readers and audiences of any era. Perhaps this sharing has encouraged some critics to imply that Shakespeare's fictional creations are almost 'real' enough to live independently from the play they inhabit.

The critic with whom the expression 'character study' is most associated is A C Bradley, who delivered a course of lectures at Oxford University which were published in 1904 as *Shakespearean Tragedy*. The book has never been out of print, and Bradley's approach has been hugely influential. It expressed the spirit of much nineteenth-century criticism, and it determined the form of much criticism in the twentieth.

Most of Bradley's account of the play considers the three major characters: Macbeth, Lady Macbeth and Banquo. However, he begins his first lecture by powerfully conveying the play's particular atmosphere and distinguishing it from Shakespeare's other great tragedies. Bradley considers the pace, imagery and major themes in ways that anticipate later critics whose approaches are more language-based. Some critics dismiss Bradley's approach, suggesting that he seems to be reading *Macbeth* not so much as a play for the stage as a novel written largely in verse. Certainly, Bradley seems most interested in the characters, though he finds that very few are fully delineated. Having evoked the play's distinctive atmosphere, Bradley writes:

> From this murky background stand out the two great terrible
> figures, who dwarf all the remaining characters of the drama.
> Both are sublime, and both inspire, far more than the other
> tragic heroes, the feeling of awe.

In explaining the awe which readers feel, Bradley describes Macbeth's imagination: 'This bold, ambitious man of action, has, within certain limits, the imagination of a poet', but without Hamlet's reflectiveness or Othello's 'romance of war' and 'infinity of love'. Bradley's approach leads him towards speculative biographical thoughts. For example, one of his appendix sections is entitled 'When Was the Murder of Duncan First Plotted?' In another he wonders about Macbeth's age and goes on to consider Macduff's line 'He has no children' from Act 4:

On the other hand I suppose no one ever imagined Macbeth, or on consideration, could imagine him, as more than middle-aged when the action begins. And in addition the reader may observe, if he finds it necessary, that Macbeth looks forward to having children (Act 1 Scene 7, line 72), and that his terms of endearment ('dearest love', 'dearest chuck') and his language in public ('sweet remembrancer') do not suggest that he and his wife are old; they even suggest that she at least is scarcely middle-aged. But this discussion tends to grow ludicrous.

The critic L C Knights certainly found this type of concern ludicrous and misguided. He argued that the play should be seen as a dramatic poem, and parodied Bradley's approach in his article, 'How Many Children Had Lady Macbeth?' Many modern critics agree with Knights, believing that Bradley interprets the plays too narrowly, ignoring, for example, the social and political contexts within which the tragedy occurs. Bradley has little to say about Duncan ('the kind old king') and his regime, nor about the long scene in England and Malcolm's invasion of Scotland. Much of what he writes about Macduff concerns the family and the sentimental effect of the slaughtered child. He compares that effect with children in Shakespeare's other plays.

Bradley felt that Shakespeare wrote four 'pure tragedies' (*Hamlet, Othello, King Lear* and *Macbeth*) and that they were intended to reassure the audience or reader. Bradley believes that, after great tumult, pain and loss, the plays' endings give a sense that order has been restored and that evil has been defeated. He ends his study of Macbeth's character with a hint of optimism:

> In the very depths a gleam of his native love of goodness, and with it a touch of tragic grandeur, rests upon him.

Before considering criticism that radically departs from or rejects Bradley's approach, it is helpful to identify some of the major characteristics of traditional criticism. There is, of course, great variation among the critics who might be called 'traditional', but in general they share certain assumptions:
- a concentration on the characters of Macbeth and Lady Macbeth, and what might be called their 'tragic flaw'

- a reluctance to address, in depth, political and social aspects of the play
- readings which do not challenge existing social structures
- an assumption of coherence and unity in the play, and some kind of harmony at its end
- a claim to objectivity, free from ideological bias

Though *Macbeth* dramatises personal and political disorder, many traditional critics have found it coherent as a play. Caroline Spurgeon in *Shakespeare's Imagery and What it Tells Us* (1935) identified image-clusters as a dominant feature and argued that they contributed to the distinctive atmosphere of the play. By pointing to the images of a small, ignoble man encumbered by inappropriate clothes, she questioned Bradley's view of Macbeth as an awesome character. She argued that an audience's moral judgements are supported by imagery of light standing for virtue and darkness and disease for evil and death. She finds moral force in the recurrent images of reverberating sound: 'the incalculable and boundless effects of evil in the nature of one man'. Today Spurgeon's approach is much criticised for its narrow range of interest, for its unquestioning praise of all that Shakespeare wrote, and for its efforts to identify in the imagery Shakespeare's own likes, dislikes and personality. However, her work encouraged further studies, which have demonstrated how imagery plays a distinctive part in every Shakespeare play.

Wilson Knight acknowledges his debt to Spurgeon in his influential book *The Wheel of Fire*. He too pays little attention to *Macbeth* as a play, seeing it more as a poem with interrelated themes and images. His essay 'The Metaphysic of Evil' begins, like Bradley's lecture, with the play's atmosphere of evil; he refers particularly to evidence of surprise, amazement, questions, rumours and insecure knowledge, and argues that 'fear' is the play's dominant word and feeling. Even more than Bradley, Knight sees a moral pattern, from goodness to the temporary dominance of evil followed by a return (largely through the imagery) to virtue and order:

> By 'the grace of Grace' (Act 5 Scene 9, line 39) alone Malcolm
> will restore health to Scotland. The murk, indeed, thins
> towards the end. Bright daylight dawns and the green leaves
> of Birnam come against Macbeth. A world climbs out of its

darkness, and in the dawn that panorama below is a thing of nightmare delusion. The 'sovereign flower' (Act 5 Scene 2, line 30) is bright-dewed in the bright dawn, and the murk melts into the mists of morning: the Child is crowned, the Tree of Life in his hand.

In another essay Knight sees the evil in *Macbeth* in relation to 'life themes': '(i) Human Values, Warrior Honour and Imperial Sway; (ii) Human Nature, sleep and feasting; (iii) Pure Nature – animals, birds, winds, sun and stars'. Knight claims to show how all of these conflict with their opposites or are subject to parody. He argues that Macbeth himself retains some of these values, even at the end, when he dies with a courage reminiscent of the former Thane of Cawdor. Knight believes that evil is bound to be temporary because 'absolute disorder prohibits self-consistency: it helps to slay itself'. The essay's last sentence repeats Knight's emphasis on imagery of children: 'The baby-peace is crowned.'

Few subsequent critics share Knight's Christian optimism. Wilbur Sanders explores what he sees as the play's strong pessimism, and in his essay 'An Unknown Fear' he devotes much attention to the play's second half, which some earlier critics have felt to lack the vivid excitement of Acts 1 and 2. Sanders explores 'Macbeth's fierce brand of nihilism' and his awesome ability to face the horrors that he has allowed into his mind. The victory of Malcolm and Macduff is a necessary moral triumph, but Sanders finds little imaginative power in it. At the end, he feels, 'we are left with an awed sense of the overwhelming potency and vitality of evil'.

Throughout the twentieth century there were a growing number of interpretations of *Macbeth* which acknowledged uncertainty and pessimism and which did not assume artistic tidiness. Critics also explored the cultural context of Shakespeare's writing and found it to be much more complicated than Tillyard had argued in *The Elizabethan World Picture* (1943). Tillyard described a cosmic hierarchy which the Elizabethans inherited from the Middle Ages. All creation was ranged in a fixed order from the angels to men to beasts and plants. This 'world picture' was variously regarded as a chain of being, a network of correspondences and a cosmic dance. Tillyard argued that the chaos let loose in *Macbeth* makes its powerful impact only when seen in contrast to the ideal of harmony. His argument attracted much support for a while, but is rejected today as a gross oversimplification of Elizabethan (or Jacobean) beliefs.

Modern criticism

Throughout the second half of the twentieth century and in the twenty-first, critical approaches to Shakespeare have radically challenged the traditional assumptions described above. New approaches argue that traditional interpretations focus too much on character and ignore history, society and cultural contexts. This detachment from the real world is seen to make them elitist, sexist and unpolitical. Modern criticism also concerns itself with how changing social assumptions at different periods of time have affected interpretations of the play.

Contemporary perspectives include many different, and often conflicting, approaches, but share some common features. Modern criticism:

- is sceptical of character approaches, but often uses them;
- concentrates on political, social and economic factors (arguing that these factors determine Shakespeare's creativity and the interpretations of audiences and critics);
- identifies contradictions, fragmentation and disunity in the plays;
- questions the possibility of 'happy' or 'hopeful' endings, preferring ambiguous or sombre endings;
- produces readings that are subversive of existing social structures;
- identifies how the plays express the interests of dominant groups, particularly rich and powerful males;
- insists that 'theory' (psychological, social, etc.) is essential to produce valid readings;
- often expresses its commitment (for example, to feminism, equality or political change);
- argues that all readings are political or ideological (and that traditional criticism falsely claims to be objective);
- argues that traditional approaches have always interpreted Shakespeare conservatively, in ways that maintain the interests of the elite, dominant class.

Political criticism

'Political criticism' is a convenient label for approaches concerned with power and social structure in the world of the play and how they reflect Shakespeare's world and today's. Shakespeare's tragedies and histories in particular have invited much perceptive variety from critics who take this approach.

Political interpretations oppose Tillyard's 'great chain of being' (see page 96), which, according to J W Lever, saw Jacobean theatre as 'a place of drawn curtains and stopped clocks'. He and Victor Kiernan, a Marxist critic, argue that attitudes were changing in Shakespeare's time. There was much dissent from King James's beliefs in Church and state. They point to the difficulties in controlling political and social turbulence surrounding King James's accession, and to the newly emerging and aspiring middle classes, the rise of individualism and the Puritan movement. Lever argues that playwrights often expressed contemporary protest against absolute monarchy and against the increasing powers of the state, with its use of lawyers and secret agents to suppress dissident opinion.

A play exists both at the time of its writing and afterwards as different performances of it in constantly changing times. Therefore political critics interpret the play as a product of the social, economic and political structures of both Shakespeare's era and of the critic's own times. Jan Kott, the influential Polish critic, titled his book *Shakespeare Our Contemporary*. He finds parallels between the violence and cruelty of the modern world (especially from his own experiences of resisting the Nazis in Poland) and the worlds of tyranny and despair that Shakespeare depicted in his tragedies. Kott argues that history, rather than fate or the gods, is the cause of tragedy. He uses the image of 'the Grand Mechanism' of history: a great staircase up which characters tread to their doom, each step 'marked by murder, perfidy, treachery'. It does not matter if a character is good or bad, history will overwhelm them. Characters have little or no power over their lives, but are swept aside by inevitable social and historical forces beyond their control.

Kott argues that the Grand Mechanism in the plot of *Macbeth* operates through the clinical logic of a murderer who then 'must' continue to kill before being killed. However, Kott feels this cycle of murder does not possess the logic of a mechanism but works through nightmare, which paralyses and terrifies. He compares murder to the loss of virginity: by killing Duncan Macbeth crosses the threshold of a new world, which Kott calls the 'Auschwitz experience'. Kott does not see the play as a psychological study of nightmare within an individual mind: he rejects nineteenth-century interpretations of character.

Instead he compares Macbeth's language of ambiguity and negation to that of the existentialists, who deny that the universe has in-built meaning or purpose, and who require individuals to take responsibility for their own actions and destinies. In a bleak view of the social world of *Macbeth*, Kott concludes: 'Macbeth is unable to blow the world up. But he can go on murdering to the end.'

Other examples of 'political' approaches to *Macbeth* include:

- Established order is insecure both at the beginning and the end of the play. Alan Sinfield believes that there is a dangerous split between legitimate rule and actual power. In Act 1 Duncan relies heavily on Macbeth; in Act 5 Malcolm's success owes much to Macduff, the king-maker. Therefore Shakespeare may be suggesting that a cycle of rivalry and violent usurpation will continue.
- Duncan is far from being an ideal king: he relies heavily on others; he is too trusting; his state is in danger before Macbeth murders him; his appointment of Malcolm as heir is illegal in an elective system of monarchy. Therefore there is much doubt about Malcolm's claim to the throne (see page 76). Some critics see Duncan's apparent warmth and benevolence merely as effective public relations to make his political decisions more acceptable.
- Duncan legitimises extreme violence in Act 1 when it is used against enemies of his regime. Macbeth behaves in a similar way when trying to achieve security as king. This leads political critics to be sceptical about any clear distinction between Duncan as representing good and Macbeth as evil.
- Though the play focuses chiefly on kings and the nobility, there are also some characters from the lower classes. Kiernan concentrates on the social conditions of Shakespeare's time, and suggests that the Messenger, the Old Man and the bewildered grooms show gleams of humanity in a dark play.
- In Act 4 Scene 3 Macduff speaks of fighting against Macbeth's evil, but in the interests of political necessity, he is prepared to tolerate the many kinds of villainy that Malcolm describes.
- The play begins with Sweno's failed invasion. It ends with a successful invasion from England with Edward the Confessor's support that establishes Malcolm as king. Some critics who take a political approach compare Edward's support with the Pope's excommunication of Queen Elizabeth. For much of her reign she

was threatened by invasion from an alliance of Catholic European powers. A Jacobean audience might be uneasy about the legitimacy of invasion.

- Political critics reject the notion of personified or abstract evil at work in the play, arguing that the deaths and disruptions it portrays spring solely from the actions of human beings who are themselves the products of an unjust and violent society.

A major political issue is that of King James's belief in the divine right of kings (see page 79). Sinfield argues much of his political case through Buchanan's *History of Scotland*, one of Shakespeare's possible sources, and a text which angered King James. Buchanan believed that sovereignty derives from the people and that the troubles in Scotland historically sprang not from unruly people but from unruly monarchs, who aimed for 'an absolute and lawless despotism'. If *Macbeth* owes much to Buchanan's beliefs, then the play is likely to be sceptical about the rights of all the kings (Duncan, Macbeth, Malcolm – and King James himself) when they follow Macduff's advice to Malcolm: 'But fear not yet / To take upon you what is yours'.

Feminist criticism

Feminist criticism is part of the wider project of feminism, which aims to achieve rights and equality for women in social, political and economic life. It challenges sexism: those beliefs and practices which result in the degradation, oppression and subordination of women. Feminist criticism therefore challenges traditional portrayals of women characters as examples of 'virtue' or 'vice'. It rejects 'male ownership' of criticism in which men determined what questions were to be asked of a play, and which answers were acceptable.

A traditional view of *Macbeth* raises few questions about a male-dominated society in which females are subordinate to the warlike culture. Domestic life (based on female values) is seen as far less important than warfare and politics, from which women are excluded. A traditional critical approach argues that Scotland's contamination is associated with deviant women: the Witches are ambiguous in their gender, and Lady Macbeth abandons her feminine nature to assume the male values of ambition and ferocity. At the end of the play Malcolm makes an orthodox male judgement on the two criminals: Macbeth is a 'butcher' but his wife has violated deeper values and is therefore 'fiend-like'. Lady Macduff is the only woman to uphold orthodox views.

The two men who rescue Scotland have, in their different ways, escaped the taint. Malcolm declares that he is a virgin: 'I am yet / Unknown to woman'. His mother (who 'Died every day she lived') seems to have lived in prayer and penance almost like a nun. Macduff was ripped from his mother's womb, and therefore did not pass through the genital area of female 'contamination'.

Feminist critics challenge such interpretations and the assumptions that lie behind them. In *Suffocating Mothers*, Janet Adelman argues that Macbeth is weak because he is insecure about his male identity. He wishes to escape from a destructive maternal power that Lady Macbeth tries to suppress in herself. In murdering Duncan, Macbeth destroys both the 'father' principles of authority, lineage and honour, and also those 'mother' aspects of growth and nurture that the vulnerable king expresses in Act 1 Scene 6. In Act 2 Macbeth sees himself as the rapist Tarquin, and Duncan as the female victim, Lucretia. After the murder, Duncan's corpse will assume a female power and become the Gorgon that destroys sight: the male sight of the sons, who therefore have no power to act in a traditional male way, but flee the country instead.

Adelman sees Macduff as an ambivalent figure. When he hears of his wife's death, he reacts in a fully human way. Male toughness, in the form of revenge, is appropriate, but prior to this Macduff felt the 'female' response: the quiet and private submission to grief, acknowledging the value of tenderness. He criticises Malcolm for trying to push him immediately into stereotypical male anger. However, Macduff also left his wife and family to their fate, a decision he never fully explains. Adelman argues that, like Macbeth, Macduff is in some way evading the claims of the woman, and that this instinct to escape continued to be present from his unnatural birth, finally allowing him to fulfil the prophecy and destroy Macbeth.

Other feminist critics point out that most of the play's families are deprived of either women or children. Duncan, Banquo and Siward do not mention wives but only male children to be seen as heirs to perpetuate the male culture. Macbeth and his wife refer to children but appear to be childless, and Macduff abandons his wife and child.

Juliet Dusinberre in *Shakespeare and the Nature of Women* writes of the extreme difference between Lady Macduff and Lady Macbeth when faced with 'the inattentive male world'. Macduff told his wife nothing about his plans for England, because

> in politics power hangs on the power to inflict injury. Women are not told events because they cannot alter them. Women parry powerlessness by becoming adept plotters, channelling into premeditation the energy which men expend in performance. Feminine cunning is proverbial.

Patriarchal male society, in which men are all-powerful, excludes the Witches even further than normal women from the centre of influence. Some feminist critics argue that witchcraft is more a convenient myth than a truth; 'witch' is simply a label suggesting foulness, with which male authority can denigrate an opponent. Terry Eagleton suggests that the Witches are the play's real heroines:

> As the most fertile force in the play, the Witches inhabit an anarchic, richly ambiguous zone both in and out of official society: they live in their own world but intersect with Macbeth's. They are poets, prophetesses and devotees of the female cult, radical separatists who scorn male power and lay bare the hollow sound and fury at its core.

One feminist production presented the Witches as colourful, charismatic survivors, exuberantly free of traditional male restraints and limitations. Productions that bring the Witches onstage at the end are able to emphasise the irony that their predictions are fulfilled and that, in a sense, the male future is in the hands of these despised female outcasts.

Performance criticism
Performance criticism fully acknowledges that *Macbeth* is a play: a script to be performed by actors to an audience. It examines all aspects of the play in performance: its staging in the theatre or on film and video. Performance criticism focuses on Shakespeare's stagecraft and the semiotics of theatre (signs: words, costumes, gestures, etc.) together with the 'afterlife' of the play (what happened to *Macbeth* after Shakespeare wrote it). That involves scrutiny of how productions at different periods have presented the play. As such, performance

criticism appraises how the text has been cut, added to, rewritten and rearranged to present a version felt appropriate to the times.

Macbeth has always been a popular play onstage and has often been used in parodies and imitations. Certain lines are frequently quoted: 'Out, damned spot'; 'Tomorrow, and tomorrow, and tomorrow'. Events and characters have entered popular culture, such as the Witches and Banquo's Ghost. In the nineteenth century, many Romantic writers and artists were inspired by Shakespeare, notably the Italian composer Giuseppe Verdi. He had seen impressive stage performances, and his opera of *Macbeth* (1847) follows contemporary interest in elaborate stage design, with large-scale scenes for the Witches and a prominence for Lady Macbeth that is stronger than in Shakespeare's original. The play has made a powerful impact on film, with notable versions by directors such as Orson Welles (1948), Roman Polanski (1971) and Trevor Nunn (1978). One of the most compelling adaptations was made in 1957 when Akira Kurosawa set his *Throne of Blood* in medieval Japanese samurai culture.

The first recorded description of a performance was by Simon Forman, a doctor and astrologer, who saw *Macbeth* at The Globe in 1611. He summarises much of the story and he was clearly moved by the banquet scene, but he includes some eccentric, and perhaps inaccurate, detail about how the Witches appeared and about Macbeth and Banquo 'riding through a wood'. It is widely thought today that the text of *Macbeth* was altered or added to soon after Shakespeare wrote it in 1606. The playwright Thomas Middleton was, to some extent, a collaborator on the Witches' scenes. He is believed to have revised the play in 1610–11 and wrote his own play, *The Witch*, a few years later, using the same songs in both plays.

Macbeth went through further transformation after the Restoration of Charles II in 1660. Playwrights of that time valued Shakespeare, but many felt that he needed 'rescuing' from the flaws in his plays, which were thought to be products of the 'barbarous' age in which he lived. Many of his plays were adapted to 'improve' the stagecraft and to clarify the moral lessons. Most modern critics feel that these revisions, by removing some of the ambiguities and inelegancies of style, gave the revisions an unShakespearean blandness.

The main reviser of *Macbeth* was Sir William Davenant, who claimed to be Shakespeare's godson (or his actual son). His version was published in 1674 and continued to be the standard theatre script until the mid-eighteenth century, when the great actor David Garrick restored much of Shakespeare's version, but also made adaptations of his own, including a bombastic death speech for Macbeth.

Davenant added much song and dance to the Witches' scenes, perhaps responding to the interest in opera at this time. He made the play more simply a warning about Macbeth's ambition and tyranny, rather than exploring a metaphysical evil. Davenant, writing soon after the Civil War, emphasised this strong political dimension by developing Macduff's character in extra scenes which also debate his political motives. Lady Macbeth's role is also enlarged, thus answering the problem that many actors have expressed about her long absence between the banquet and her sleepwalking. Edith Evans, in the early twentieth century, refused to play the part because, she complained, 'there is a page missing' in Shakespeare's script.

Many productions in the 150 years after the Restoration had the Witches played by the company's comic actors; sometimes their numbers swelled into a *corps de ballet*, and in an 1864 production 100 actors took part in their songs and dances. Many nineteenth- and early twentieth-century interpretations have made the Witches' scenes visually impressive, often with a gloomy Gothic beauty. Edward Gordon Craig had Macbeth descending in Act 4 to a deep pit that appeared like an underground cathedral. Sometimes the apparitions have been gigantic puppets dwarfing Macbeth.

Some notable twentieth-century productions have taken an opposite line, as when 'the Witches became part of a grey mass of suffering populace'. Interpretations of the first scene have seen them creep out from amongst the battlefield corpses; in Act 1 Scene 3 they have obscured themselves as boulders or other natural features and grown into the scene as from the earth. Some directors show them as slightly and infrequently as possible, so suggesting that they exist chiefly as figments of Macbeth's mind. In one production Macbeth lies in bed with his wife and dreams his Act 4 Scene 1 visit to the Witches and the prophecies they make for him. In another version the Witches could assume almost any identity, simply by raising a black cloak. Thus, characters like Ross and the Captain could seem to merge with the 'characters' of the Witches.

Throughout the history of the play in performance, the Witches have been presented in vastly different ways: as men, disgusting old crones, stylish entertainers, naked young women. A recent feminist interpretation sees them as a troupe of players, colourful, versatile, energetic, able to adopt various disguises and roles, instigating the story and leading the audience towards the hero ('there to meet with Macbeth'). Often, in sceptical times, directors have felt that the traditional trappings of witchcraft will have little effect on audiences, and have therefore searched for an expression of evil that they consider more relevant to their times, as in the 1936 'voodoo' *Macbeth*, when Orson Welles set his stage production in the Caribbean.

The relationship between Macbeth and his wife is so fundamental to any production that some actors have found limited appeal in the play because, apart from the two 'stars', the characterisation appears to them shallow and perfunctory. Macbeth has wide-ranging relationships: with soldiers, servants, noblemen and within his own conscience. In contrast, Lady Macbeth relates only to her husband. Therefore she has acquired a sense of mystery, inviting different actors to bring out (or supply) various roles and functions. She has been sensual, socially ambitious, demonically possessed, a child-wife, maternal in soothing her husband's neuroses, and 'a terrible woman' intent on mastering and 'draining' a prominent man. Some interpretations have recalled original sin, whereby the serpent-linked devil, through the Witches, infects the woman (Eve / Lady Macbeth), who then infects and destroys the man, and with him the entire male-dominated social and political structure.

Many productions express positive values in the Macbeths' marriage partly complementing the evils they commit. There is often dignity, grandeur, compassion and pathos in such productions. Laurence Olivier and Vivien Leigh, playing the roles in the 1950s, reminded one critic 'that Macbeth and his Lady were lovers before they were criminals'.

The twentieth century also saw a return to simpler stagings of the play. Under the influence of William Poel and Harley Granville-Barker, the Shakespearean stage in general was cleared of historical clutter. The aim was to minimise theatrical illusion and return to the plainer values of the Elizabethan bare stage. Trevor Nunn's production for the RSC in 1976–8 was a fine example of powerful simplicity. The play was set in what was more like a rehearsal studio than a formal theatre. Actors sat on packing cases round a chalk circle concentrating on the centre, often simply awaiting their moment to perform. There were no magical effects, but nonetheless a frightening sense of a mysterious evil beyond the circle. Within the playing area the characters behaved in low-key, 'normal' ways, taking evident responsibility for their actions.

Psychoanalytic criticism

In the twentieth century, psychoanalysis became a major influence on the understanding and interpretation of human behaviour. The founder of psychoanalysis, Sigmund Freud, explained personality as the result of unconscious and irrational desires, repressed memories or wishes, sexuality, fantasy, anxiety and conflict. Freud's theories have had a strong influence on criticism and stagings of Shakespeare's plays, especially on tragedies, which dramatise violent and erratic behaviour.

Several psychoanalytic studies of *Macbeth* focus on Lady Macbeth. Freud himself wrote a brief study on her, speculating on the couple's childless state, but rejecting this as the cause for both characters' changed personalities in the play's second half. Freud finds that the economy of time in the action of the tragedy precludes much of his investigation, but proposes the theory that husband and wife may be two halves of a single 'psychic individuality'. This seems little more than the suggestion that each character can be understood only in relation to the other.

Janet Adelman (see page 101) combines a psychoanalytic with a feminist reading of the play. She argues that the play dramatises a fear of female coercion, proposed cosmically by the Witches in the first scene, then located within society by Lady Macbeth. In this reading, Adelman interprets 'take my milk for gall' (Act 1 Scene 5, line 46) as 'take my milk *as* gall'. Thus, something demonic threatens men within their culture and the action of the play contains the fantasy of vulnerable 'men-children' trying to escape from their birth and nurturing by women.

Psychoanalytic criticism has also explored:
- notions of manhood and manliness in a male culture, suggesting that ceremonies in peace and brutality in war are both assertive ways of challenging inner vulnerability;
- witchcraft: not so much the psychology of the witch, but the collective psychology of a male culture that excludes or even demonises unconventional behaviour;

- the Witches as 'mother', instigating Macbeth's crimes;
- Lady Macbeth as a figure of repression, as 'castrator' of Macbeth, as 'overpowering mother', and as the projection of Macbeth's wishes for kingship;
- Macbeth as Duncan's 'son', harbouring an Oedipal wish to kill his 'father'.

But psychoanalytic theories have obvious weaknesses: they cannot be proved or disproved and they largely neglect historical and social factors which are crucial to a full understanding of the play. Psychoanalytic approaches are therefore often accused of bringing theory to the play, rather than arriving at theory from close scrutiny of Shakespeare's text. But *Macbeth* offers rich opportunities for psychoanalytic interpretation because it is so clearly concerned with access to the inner mind, fractured personality, broken relationships and supernatural interventions that have the quality of nightmares, omens and prophecies.

Postmodern criticism

Postmodern criticism (sometimes called 'deconstruction') is not always easy to understand because it is not centrally concerned with consistency or reasoned argument. For example, such critical approaches regard the play's characters as 'textual arrangements' that express ideas about people, whereas traditional criticism assumes that the characters, though fictional, should be regarded as persons. Postmodern critics do not accept that one section of the story is necessarily connected to what follows nor even that there is stability in the meaning of words. They claim that words simply refer to other words, and so any interpretation is constantly delayed. In contrast, traditional critics look for coherence as a sign of quality in the play: coherence in character motivation, image patterns, themes, structure. Where traditionalists aim to explain away awkward points and help the text into coherence, the postmodernists welcome disjunctions and find richness in the fragmentation of a text.

Because of such assumptions, postmodern criticism is sometimes described as 'reading against the grain' or as 'textual harassment'. The approach therefore has obvious drawbacks in providing a model for examination students, who are expected to display reasoned, coherent argument and respect for the evidence of the text.

Postmodern approaches to *Macbeth* are most clearly seen in stage productions. There the disjunctions may be described as 'a mixture of styles'. For example, characters may be dressed in costumes from different periods, soldiers may carry both ancient and modern weapons, stage design may mingle realistic and symbolic elements. A director may urge actors to 'play each scene for itself' or even each speech for itself, welcoming as rich variety the contradictions that may result. Ironically, Shakespeare himself has been regarded as a postmodern writer for the ways he mixes genres in his plays: the appearance of the drunken Porter at a crucial moment in the tragedy; the possible comedy of Macbeth being fooled by the Ghost in the tense banquet scene.

Some postmodern views of language in *Macbeth* point to puns, riddles and prophecies, all designed to complicate and mislead, or to lie 'like truth' (Act 5 Scene 5, line 43). The play is seen to have its basis in equivocation (see page 70), a way of manipulating language whereby traitors can evade punishment. Examples of post-structuralist criticism by Malcolm Evans and Catherine Belsey can be found in Sinfield's *Casebook* (see page 127). Both are based on assumptions about the instability of human subjectivity (individual identity) and of culture and language itself. And in a postmodern reading that extends beyond language into feminist and political interpretations, Terry Eagleton argues that Shakespeare's 'belief in social stability is jeopardised by the very language in which it is articulated'. Hence he argues that the physical fluidity of the Witches and the dark playfulness of their language makes them in a sense the heroines of the play. He admits that such a reading is not to interpret the play on its own terms, but that 'reading against the grain' may help better understanding.

Organising your responses

The purpose of this section is to help you improve your writing about *Macbeth*. It offers practical guidance on two types of task: writing about an extract from the play and writing an essay. Whether you are answering an examination question, preparing coursework (term papers), or carrying out research into your own chosen topic, this section will help you organise and present your responses.

In all your writing there are three vital points to remember:

- *Macbeth* is a play. Although it is usually referred to as a 'text', *Macbeth* is not a book, but a script intended to be acted on a stage. So your writing should demonstrate that you are aware of the play in performance as theatre. That means you should always try to read (and even to direct) the play with an 'inner eye', thinking about how it could look and sound onstage.
- *Macbeth* is not a presentation of 'reality'. It is a dramatic construct in which the playwright, through theatre, engages the emotions and intellect of the audience. The audience may identify with the characters, be deeply moved by them, and think of them as if they are living human beings. However, when you write, a major part of your task is to show how Shakespeare achieves the dramatic effects that so engage his audience. When you discuss his handling of language, character, plot and themes, your writing reveals how Shakespeare gives insight into crucial moral, social and political dilemmas of his times – and yours.
- How Shakespeare learned his craft. As a schoolboy and in his early years as a playwright, Shakespeare used all kinds of models or frameworks to guide his writing. But he quickly learned how to vary and adapt the models to his own dramatic purposes. This section offers frameworks that you can use to structure your writing. As you use them, follow Shakespeare's example! Adapt them to suit your own writing style and needs.

Writing about an extract

It is an expected part of all Shakespeare study that you should be able to write well about an extract (sometimes called a 'passage') from the play. An extract is usually 30–70 lines long, and you are invited to comment on it. The instructions vary. Sometimes the task is very briefly expressed:

- Write a detailed commentary on the following passage.
  or
- Write about the effect of this extract on your own thoughts and feelings.

At other times a particular focus is specified for your writing:

- With close reference to the language and imagery of the passage, show in what ways it helps to establish important issues in the play.
  or
- Analyse the style and structure of the extract, showing what it contributes to your appreciation of the play's major concerns.

In writing your response, you must of course take account of the precise wording of the task, and ensure that you concentrate on each particular point specified. But you are always required to comment in detail on the language. You should identify and evaluate how the language:

- reveals character;
- contributes to plot development;
- offers opportunities for dramatic effect;
- embodies crucial concerns of the play as a whole (i.e. 'themes', 'issues', 'preoccupations').

The framework on page III is a guide to how you can write a detailed commentary on an extract. Writing a paragraph on each item will help you to explore the meaning of the extract and how Shakespeare achieves his effects. You should, however, regard the framework as a model to be adapted for your individual interpretation according to the emphasis you wish to give to particular features in the passage. For example, the model does not highlight 'use of verse', but you may wish to discuss the dramatic effects of Shakespeare's switching from verse to prose. Important aspects of the verse can often be discussed under the heading of 'Repetition' to show the rhythms of the extract. Sometimes 'Diction' might include references to the play's dominant motifs (for example in the recurrence of a key word or phrase), or to 'wordplay', particularly the use of puns. You will find that practice with different passages will increase your skill, and any passage set in an examination is likely to provide opportunities to write about each of the items given in the framework.

> **Paragraph 1:** Locate the extract in the play, refer to its context (i.e. what comes immediately before and after) and say who is onstage.
>
> **Paragraph 2:** State what the extract is about and identify its structure.
>
> **Paragraph 3:** Identify the mood or atmosphere of the extract.
>
> **Paragraphs 4–8:**
> Diction (vocabulary)
> Imagery
> Antithesis
> Repetition
> Lists
>
> These paragraphs analyse how Shakespeare achieves his effects. They concentrate on the language of the extract, showing the dramatic effect of each item, and how the language expresses crucial concerns of the play.
>
> **Paragraph 9:** Staging opportunities
>
> **Paragraph 10:** Conclusion

An example using the framework now follows. The framework headings (in bold) would not, of course, appear in your essay. They are presented only to help you see how the framework is used.

Extract

MALCOLM Let us seek out some desolate shade and there
   Weep our sad bosoms empty.

MACDUFF   Let us rather
   Hold fast the mortal sword and like good men
   Bestride our downfall birthdom; each new morn,
   New widows howl, new orphans cry, new sorrows   5
   Strike heaven on the face, that it resounds
   As if it felt with Scotland and yelled out
   Like syllable of dolour.

MALCOLM   What I believe, I'll wail;
   What know, believe; and what I can redress,
   As I shall find the time to friend, I will.   10
   What you have spoke, it may be so perchance.
   This tyrant, whose sole name blisters our tongues,
   Was once thought honest; you have loved him well –
   He hath not touched you yet. I am young, but something
   You may discern of him through me, and wisdom   15
   To offer up a weak, poor, innocent lamb
   T'appease an angry god.

MACDUFF I am not treacherous.

MALCOLM   But Macbeth is.
        A good and virtuous nature may recoil
        In an imperial charge. But I shall crave your pardon: 20
        That which you are, my thoughts cannot transpose;
        Angels are bright still, though the brightest fell.
        Though all things foul would wear the brows of grace,
        Yet grace must still look so.
MACDUFF   I have lost my hopes.
MALCOLM   Perchance even there where I did find my doubts.   25
        Why in that rawness left you wife and child,
        Those precious motives, those strong knots of love,
        Without leave-taking? I pray you,
        Let not my jealousies be your dishonours,
        But mine own safeties; you may be rightly just,   30
        Whatever I shall think.
MACDUFF   Bleed, bleed, poor country.
        Great tyranny, lay thou thy basis sure,
        For goodness dare not check thee; wear thou thy wrongs,
        The title is affeered. Fare thee well, lord,
        I would not be the villain that thou think'st   35
        For the whole space that's in the tyrant's grasp,
        And the rich East to boot.
MALCOLM   Be not offended.
        I speak not as in absolute fear of you:
        I think our country sinks beneath the yoke;
        It weeps, it bleeds, and each new day a gash   40
        Is added to her wounds. I think withal
        There would be hands uplifted in my right,
        And here from gracious England have I offer
        Of goodly thousands. But for all this,
        When I shall tread upon the tyrant's head,   45
        Or wear it on my sword, yet my poor country
        Shall have more vices than it had before,
        More suffer, and more sundry ways than ever,
        By him that shall succeed.
MACDUFF   What should he be?
MALCOLM   It is myself I mean – in whom I know   50
        All the particulars of vice so grafted
        That, when they shall be opened, black Macbeth

Will seem as pure as snow and the poor state
Esteem him as a lamb, being compared
With my confineless harms.

MACDUFF   Not in the legions   55
Of horrid hell can come a devil more damned
In evils to top Macbeth.

MALCOLM   I grant him bloody,
Luxurious, avaricious, false, deceitful,
Sudden, malicious, smacking of every sin
That has a name. But there's no bottom, none,   60
In my voluptuousness: your wives, your daughters,
Your matrons, and your maids could not fill up
The cistern of my lust, and my desire
All continent impediments would o'erbear
That did oppose my will. Better Macbeth,
Than such an one to reign.   *(Act 4 Scene 3, lines 1–66)*

Paragraph 1: Locate the extract in the play.
These lines open the scene in England just after Lady Macduff and her
children have been murdered. Malcolm is in self-imposed exile under
the protection of the English king, Edward the Confessor. He is in
mid-conversation with Macduff, who has left his family in danger in
order to persuade Malcolm to lead an army against Macbeth's tyranny.

Paragraph 2: State what the extract is about and identify its structure.
Audiences may expect Macduff and Malcolm to create an immediate
alliance. However, Malcolm appears to block all efforts to motivate
him. Macduff is surprised and increasingly disturbed as he listens.
Malcolm begins with a defeatist comment about weeping in a
'desolate shade' and warily casts doubt on everything Macduff says.
He is prepared to accept that Scotland is suffering, but doubts
Macduff's honesty, implying that he may be secretly in Macbeth's
service. Macduff seems unable to explain why he has been prepared to
leave his family unprotected. Malcolm makes a surprising self-
accusation, describing his own vices, which he declares to be worse
than Macbeth's. As the scene develops it becomes clear that Malcolm's
words are designed to test how Macduff will respond to each list of
vices.

Paragraph 3: Identify the mood or atmosphere of the extract.

After the frenzied horror of the previous scene, this episode feels calmer, with Malcolm living as though in retirement in England. Macduff has come from Scotland to initiate a military campaign against Macbeth, but he spends this extract chiefly listening to Malcolm. The dramatic force of the episode is based on argument and feels more intellectual than emotional. But Shakespeare creates the sense of an engaged, living dialogue by ending each speech in a half line which is completed by the next speaker.

Paragraph 4: Diction

Though the atmosphere seems calm, the vocabulary expresses how Macbeth's violence afflicts Scotland: 'desolate', 'sorrows', 'weep'. Words like 'foul', 'rawness' and 'tyranny' convey aggression and pain. Much of the language shows extremities of thought and feeling: 'howl', 'cry', 'yelled out'. The oppositions of evil and good are suggested in 'vice', 'devil', 'angels', 'an angry god'. Certain words describing vices have now lost the meaning they had for Jacobeans: 'sudden' for violent, 'luxurious' for lustful.

Paragraph 5: Imagery

The imagery chiefly depicts the conflict between good and evil. For Macduff, defending his mother country is a simple and strong virtue: good men can 'Bestride our downfall birthdom'. But Malcolm sees good and bad in more complicated terms. A man's love for his family, developed through time, creates 'strong knots'. Macbeth's tyranny is so vile that it 'blisters' the tongues of those who describe it, but he is also 'an angry god', so powerful that Malcolm, his victim, is a sacrificial 'lamb'. One of the most powerful images links earth and heaven (as Macbeth did in his soliloquy, 'If it were done . . .' (Act 1 Scene 7, line 1): Macduff says that heaven is like a person, struck on the face by 'new sorrows', yelling sounds of grief. Malcolm, pretending his own wickedness, uses a self-conscious image from gardening: 'All the particulars of vice so grafted', as though becoming vicious is a planned process. Malcolm describes the hypocrite, who, being foul, wishes to 'wear the brows of grace', one of the play's many images of clothing. Macduff, despairing when Malcolm refuses to join him, personifies 'Great tyranny', who can now 'wear' his wrongs. A notable sexual image occurs at line 63, where Malcolm implies his desire is insatiable as he claims that not all the women of Scotland could 'fill up / The cistern of my lust'.

Paragraph 6: Antithesis

There is much use of antithesis in the passage, as befits the contrast of Macbeth's Scotland with Edward's England. Macbeth is an 'angry god'; Malcolm is an 'innocent lamb'. Moral confusion leads to 'things foul' appearing like 'grace', and Malcolm predicts that 'black' Macbeth will seem like 'snow'. The contrast of Malcolm's apparent defeatism and Macduff's call to action appears in the antithesis that opens the scene: 'Let us seek out some desolate shade': 'Let us rather / Hold fast the mortal sword.' When Macduff despairs 'I have lost my hopes', Malcolm's riposte contains paradox as well as antithesis: 'Perchance even there where I did find my doubts.' From losing to finding sounds like a clear gain, but to move from hopes to doubts feels like regression.

Paragraph 7: Repetition

In his first speech Macduff stresses the continuing violence in Scotland: 'each new morn, / New widows howl, new orphans cry'. Immediately Malcolm replies with what can seem like parody: the repeated 'what' introduces a list of carefully connected verbs ('believe', 'wail', 'know', 'redress', 'will'). Macduff's speech of distress begins with repetition ('Bleed, bleed, poor country.') to introduce exclamations which ironically instruct the appalling situation to continue. Malcolm methodically describes his own reactions ('I think', 'I think withal') and Scotland's suffering ('our country sinks . . . It weeps, it bleeds'). His clinical description continues into a desolate future with the repeated 'more vices . . . More suffer . . . more sundry ways'.

Paragraph 8: Lists

When Malcolm reaches the moment for his own self-denigration, he prepares for this with a list of Macbeth's evils ('bloody, / Luxurious, avaricious, false, deceitful . . .), then, in switching to his own vices, he gives his list a sharper point by listing his victims: 'your wives, your daughters, / Your matrons, and your maids'.

Paragraph 9: Staging opportunities

Some productions create a contrast with the darkness of Scotland by playing this whole long scene in the light, suggesting the purity and stillness of King Edward's court. But there is also a strong link with the immediately preceding scene, in which the audience has just seen Lady Macduff and her children brutally murdered, and now Macduff is in the peace and safety of the English court. The grim irony of the contrast is strengthened by Malcolm's comment: 'He hath not touched you yet.' Productions often aim to reinforce the ironic link by using, for example, the effect of a tolling bell, which can suggest a funeral in Scotland and a call to prayer in England. The scene must establish the characters of the two who will eventually rescue Scotland. So far, the play's action has given little attention to either; their reputations and significance have been stronger than their actual presence. This episode focuses more on Malcolm and an audience is likely to be puzzled in watching him because, as later lines will show, he is not speaking honestly. The actor playing Malcolm has choices. Should he play the scene with a calm stillness, suggesting the iron self-control which the next leader will need? Should he be evidently young, restless, frightened of the dangers ahead, anxious about whether or not Macduff is genuine? There are lines where Malcolm seems reassuring ('But I shall crave your pardon', 'Be not offended'); on the other hand, he is aiming to create a moment when Macduff will be deeply discouraged. In the first part of this scene there is less focus on Macduff, even though his first speech is firm and decisive. When he begins to recognise Malcolm's reluctance, is Macduff angry, upset, disappointed, puzzled, probing? His generally short speeches give an actor several valid options.

Paragraph 10: Conclusion

The critic Frank Kermode feels that this is the play's least well-written scene. It certainly contains more talk than action, and much of the talk is calculated to mislead, so tainting Malcolm with Macbeth's fault of deviousness. One answer to this criticism is to argue that it is more of a strength than a weakness, because it shows that the moral disputes in the play can't be expressed in a simple antithesis of good versus evil. The politics of the play are evident: Malcolm will need some of Macbeth's own methods if he is to defeat him. A director of the play will need to consider whether this scene reassures the audience that Scotland will soon be in the hands of two moral and steadfast leaders, or whether it raises unanswered moral questions that will undercut the sense of triumph and relief when Macbeth is overthrown.

Writing an essay

As part of your study of *Macbeth* you will be asked to write essays, either under exam conditions or for coursework (term papers). Examinations mean that you are under pressure of time, usually having about one hour to prepare and write each essay. Coursework means that you have much longer to think about and produce your essay. But whatever the type of essay, each will require you to develop an argument about a particular aspect of *Macbeth*.

Before suggesting a strategy for your essay-writing, it is helpful to recall just what an essay is. Essay comes from the French *essai*: 'an attempt' or 'a trial'. It was originally used by the sixteenth-century French writer Montaigne (whose work Shakespeare certainly read). Montaigne used *essais* to explore particular subjects, such as friendship or cannibals or education. In each essay he used many practical examples to test his response to the topic. Soliloquies may be said to resemble Montaigne's *essais* in that they reveal the inner workings of a character's mind as he thinks his way through a problem.

The essays you write on *Macbeth* similarly require that you set out your thoughts on a particular aspect of the play, using evidence from the text. The people who read your essays (examiners, teachers, lecturers) will have certain expectations of your writing. In each essay they will expect you to discuss and analyse a particular topic, using evidence from the play to develop an argument in an organised, coherent and persuasive way. Examiners look for, and reward, what they call 'an informed personal response'. This simply means that you show you have good knowledge of the play ('informed') and can use evidence from it to support and justify your own viewpoint ('personal').

You can write about *Macbeth* from different points of view. As pages 91–109 show, you can approach the play from a number of critical perspectives (feminist, psychoanalytic, political, etc.). You can also set the play in its social, literary, political and other contexts. You should write at different levels, moving beyond description to analysis and evaluation. Simply telling the story or describing the characters is not as effective as analysing how events or characters embody wider concerns of the play. In *Macbeth*, these 'wider concerns' (themes, issues, preoccupations, or more simply, 'what the play is about') include kingship, prophecy, witchcraft and the nature of evil.

How should you answer an examination question or write a coursework essay? The following threefold structure can help you organise your response:

Opening paragraph
Developing paragraphs
Concluding paragraph.

Opening paragraph. Begin with a paragraph identifying just what topic or issue you will focus on. Show that you have understood what the question is about. You probably will have prepared for several topics. But look closely at the question and identify key words to see what particular aspect it asks you to write about. Adapt your material to answer that question. Examiners do not reward an essay, however well written, if it is not on the question set.

Developing paragraphs. This is the main body of your essay. In it you develop your argument, point by point, paragraph by paragraph. Use evidence from the play that illuminates your argument. Each paragraph makes a point of dramatic or thematic significance. Some paragraphs could make points concerned with context or particular critical approaches. The effect of your argument builds up as each paragraph adds to the persuasive quality of your essay. Use brief quotations that support your argument, and show clearly why they are relevant. Your essay should demonstrate that you are aware that *Macbeth* is a play – a drama intended for performance – and therefore open to a wide variety of interpretations and audience responses.

Concluding paragraph. Your final paragraph pulls together your main conclusions. It does not simply repeat what you have written earlier, but summarises concisely how your essay has successfully answered the question.

Example

The following notes show the 'ingredients' of an answer, given here in note form. In an examination it is usually helpful to prepare similar notes from which you write your essay, paragraph by paragraph. Remember that examiners are not impressed by 'name-dropping': use of critics' names without showing relevance to your point. They want you to show your knowledge and judgement of the play and its contexts, and how it has been interpreted from different critical perspectives.

Question: How does *Macbeth* explore the nature of evil?

Opening paragraph

- Many critics have seen the play as a moral exploration, and have identified evil as a major theme.
- *Macbeth* certainly shows evil being done, because 'evil' implies 'good' as its opposite and means something that is wicked, deeply wrong or deliberately harmful – and that is certainly evident in the play.
- But the play's exploration of the nature of evil is complex because it is carried out at three interrelated levels:
  - individual: what characters do, think and feel
  - social and political: the consequences for Scotland
  - supernatural: cosmic and metaphysical: the Witches, imagery, etc.

Developing paragraphs

The paragraphs that follow should use the framework you establish in your opening paragraph: how evil is explored at individual, social and political, and supernatural levels. Each 'level' will probably contain two or more paragraphs. Use brief quotations where possible, but in an examination only identify them by describing the scene in which they appear (e.g. the scene in the English court, rather than Act 4 Scene 3). Aim to give your essay a natural flow in which one paragraph leads to, or is linked with, the following paragraph.

- Individual (a paragraph on each of the following):
  - What Macbeth does: his evil actions in murdering Duncan (a guest, kinsman, king) and Macduff's family (innocent victims).
  - What Lady Macbeth does: calls on spirits to fill her with evil ('murdering ministers'), persuades Macbeth to murder Duncan (willing to dash out her own baby's brains).
  - What Macbeth thinks and feels: his inner struggle, uncertainty and sense of horror. Shakespeare shows him as aware of, and grappling with, evil (e.g. in his soliloquy at the banquet for Duncan).

- The effect of their evil actions on Macbeth and Lady Macbeth. After killing Duncan, Macbeth is immediately aware of, and tormented by, the evil he has done ('murder sleep'). His torment increases through the play ('O, full of scorpions is my mind') and he recognises what his evil actions have cost him (Life as 'a tale / Told by an idiot, full of sound and fury / Signifying nothing'). Lady Macbeth, having first embraced evil, declines into mental derangement ('nought's had, all's spent') and her sleepwalking scene shows the torturing consequences of her malignant intentions and urgings.
- Other characters: Banquo is tempted, but resists evil. Malcolm pretends to be evil to test Macduff's loyalty. The Murderers are simply evil agents, unthinking, unperturbed by their villainy.
- Social and political:
  - Duncan may be praised as 'good', but his regime seems based on the evil of violence and bloodshed (e.g. his praise of the Captain's speech).
  - Scotland becomes a place of tyranny under Macbeth, where cruelty and evil flourish (as reported in the scene in the English court: 'our country sinks beneath the yoke').
- Supernatural:
  - The Witches: they declare 'Fair is foul, and foul is fair', tell of evil deeds (sailor/Aleppo), prepare horrible ingredients for the cauldron, are called 'juggling fiends'. But are they evil? Or do they tempt Macbeth into choosing evil? (Many Jacobeans saw witches as evil, but the play gives scope for other interpretations).
  - Cosmic: violations of nature suggest evil as the 'horrid deed' in Macbeth's soliloquy as he thinks of killing King Duncan (which evokes the 'trumpet-tongued' protest of angels), and the unnatural prodigies described by Ross and the Old Man after Duncan's murder ('horses ate each other'). Macbeth's demand that the Witches tell him the future ('nature's germen tumble altogether').
  - Imagery: evil is suggested in the pervading imagery of darkness, predatory and mutilated animals, disease ('night's black agents to their preys do rouse', etc.).

Concluding paragraph

Write several sentences drawing together your conclusions. Try to include something fresh (e.g. from performance history, theatrical potential or contexts) which gives additional force to your argument.

- Shakespeare's exploration of evil is more complex than a simple morality play battleground of good versus evil.
- The play can end with different emphases in different performances (e.g. characters responding to their triumph over evil; the Polanski film showing that evil is likely to continue as Donaldbain visits the Witches).
- Many modern critics are sceptical about interpreting evil as an abstract concept. It is the result of human action.
- Return to the first paragraph to indicate that the play is a story about human temptations and cruelties, of wicked actions and their effects.
- The three levels are interrelated, and the play is open to interpretation: whether Macbeth chooses evil or is inexorably drawn into it.

Writing about character

As the Traditional criticism section showed (see pages 91–6), much critical writing about *Macbeth* focused on characters, responding to them as if they were living human beings. Today it is not sufficient just to describe their personalities. When you write about characters you will also be expected to show that they are dramatic constructs. That means that they embody the wider concerns of the play, have certain dramatic functions and are set in a social and political world with particular values and beliefs. For example:

- Macduff can be seen as a husband and a father with family responsibilities, and perhaps as a flawed personality, but his presence and actions also reminded Jacobean audiences of the miracle play *The Harrowing of Hell* and so anticipate his symbolic Christlike role in rescuing souls imprisoned by the devil (see page 65).
- When Macbeth invites his guests to sit down at the start of the banquet scene and refers to 'our hostess' who 'keeps her state', the significance is not only the anxious and hypocritical behaviour of husband and wife at this moment but also the function of feasts in traditional cultures. When Macbeth visits the Witches in Act 4 they

become the hosts, reminiscent of his role in the banquet he gave for Duncan and the banquet at which Banquo's ghost appears.

Many critics have felt that *Macbeth* gains much of its power not so much from the characters as, for example, from its language as a dramatic poem (see page 94) or its treatment of gender issues (see page 100) or its insights into kingship and political structures (see page 97). However, there is a danger, while writing about these issues, of seeming to reduce the characters' importance. The play was written for performance and actors who play the characters will naturally aim to express the traits of personality that they find in the script. Characters are dramatic constructs, but in performance they can become vividly experienced, almost real presences. Therefore, when you write about *Macbeth*, you should also respond to each character's thoughts, feelings and behaviour.

Macbeth is a military hero, a criminal and a deeply sensitive individual. As such he elicits mixed responses from an audience, and actors will choose between the extremes of alienating an audience with brutality and horror and evoking sympathy for his suffering. Both as general and king Macbeth plays prominent public roles, but much of the drama occurs within his mind. He is tempted to evil deeds by a mixture of the Witches' suggestions, his wife's pressure and his own fascination with sacrilegious murder. He understands that he will be punished both politically and by his conscience. From Act 3, he struggles to harden his responses and lose 'the taste of fears'. Different interpretations of Macbeth can vary between showing his final moments as heroic, isolated endurance or the snarling of a trapped animal.

Reading an actor's account of playing the role can help your writing. For example, Derek Jacobi (see Robert Smallwood, page 127) says about Macbeth at his soliloquy in Act 1 Scene 7: 'He is a highly intelligent, imaginative, articulate man, quite unlike the brutal non-thinking slasher of the battlefield, the tried and tested killing machine. Here we are in contact with that other side of him, the great contrast with his life as a soldier . . . His head is full of the mixture of good and evil. At this moment the evil side of him, which we all possess, is getting the upper hand and in order to balance it, he brings up the best, the purest, the most innocent of images, of angels, and new-born babies, the sky . . . on the other side are the dark, blood-driven, evil, dark thoughts. Eventually in this soliloquy he chooses good: the good images win – until Lady Macbeth comes in and taunts his manliness.'

Lady Macbeth has close contact only with her husband. She does not foresee the consequences of their criminal acts and this ignorance helps to sustain her powerful focus on him and their 'great quell'. When in Act 3 she begins to understand the emptiness of their achievement and sees Macbeth moving away from her into his own thoughts, she despairs. Shakespeare does not show Lady Macbeth's decline into nervous breakdown and eventual suicide, apart from one glimpse of the horrifying process: the torment of her sleepwalking.

A director's viewpoint can also help your writing. For example, here is advice I have offered to Lady Macbeth at Act 3 Scene 2: 'After the previous public scene, this is a private scene and she might expect her close relationship with Macbeth to remain unchanged. But her usual dominant spirit is missing. Servants seem better informed than she is. Alone, she admits truths in lines 4–7 ('Nought's had, all's spent . . .') that had never crossed her mind before. This shaky start conditions the rest of the scene. When Macbeth appears, she pleads rather than asserts: she speaks of his being alone probably because she has begun to feel lonely herself. She is puzzled by unfamiliar misgivings, she feels drained of energy and so becomes an audience to Macbeth's words rather than his partner. She is as much alarmed by her own state of mind as she is transfixed by his intensity.'

Supporting characters seem less developed than those in Shakespeare's other major tragedies. **Duncan** appears only in Act 1 and presents a humanised type of kingship in the context of rebellion and warfare. **Banquo** expresses a watchful restraint, seems suspicious of Macbeth and is killed in Act 3. His personality has been variously interpreted, ranging from high integrity to deviousness and timid indecision. **Macduff** behaves with reckless independence of Macbeth's regime and becomes the toughest of his opponents, but also shows tenderness in his grief when hearing of his family's slaughter. **Malcolm**, who is not given dramatic focus until Act 4, has been seen as a moral avenger or a pragmatic manipulator.

As always, never forget that *Macbeth* is a play to be acted before it is a script to be read. Shakespeare's language gives actors many opportunities to play characters in different ways. In your writing you should try to achieve a balance between analysing personality as though the characters have an independent life and seeing them in their social, critical and dramatic contexts.

A note on examiners

Examiners do not try to trap or trick you. They set questions and select passages for comment intended to help you write your own informed personal response to the play. They expect your answer to display a sound knowledge and understanding of the play, and to be well structured. They want you to develop an argument, using evidence from the text to support your interpretations and judgements. Examiners know there is never one 'right answer' to a question, but always opportunities to explore different approaches and interpretations. As such, they welcome answers which directly address the question set, but which show originality, insight and awareness of complexity. Above all, they reward responses which show your awareness that *Macbeth* is a play for performance, and which demonstrate that you can identify how Shakespeare achieves his dramatic effects.

And what about critics? Examiners want you to show you are aware of different critical approaches to the play. But they do not expect you simply to drop critics' names into your essay, or to remember quotations from critics. Rather, they want you to show that you can interpret the play from different critical perspectives, and that you know that any critical approach provides only a partial view of *Macbeth*. Often, that need only be just a section of your essay. Examiners are always interested in your view of the play. They expect your writing to show how you have come to that view from thinking critically about the play, reading it, seeing it performed, reading about it, and perhaps from acting some of it yourself – even if that acting is in your imagination!

Resources

Books

Janet Adelman, *Suffocating Mothers*, Routledge, 1992
A stimulating feminist view of several Shakespeare plays. The chapter on *Macbeth* discusses the impact of Lady Macbeth and the Witches on the hero's struggle for his male identity.

Jonathan Bate, *The Genius of Shakespeare*, Picador, 1997
Explores the development of Shakespeare's reputation, including a fascinating discussion of the Romantic artist Fuseli's images of *Macbeth*.

John Bayley, *Shakespeare and Tragedy*, Routledge, 1981
Includes an essay on *Macbeth* in the chapter 'Tragedy and Consciousness'.

A C Bradley, *Shakespearean Tragedy*, Penguin, 1991
First published in 1904. A very useful analysis of character, especially of Macbeth and Lady Macbeth. Also examines the power of the language and the 'grandeur' of the tragedy.

Cleanth Brooks, *The Well Wrought Urn*, Harcourt, Brace, 1947
A chapter entitled 'The Naked Babe and the Cloak of Manliness' explores these two powerful metaphors and considers their depth, paradoxes and resonance through the play.

Dympna Callaghan, Lorraine Helms, and Jyotsna Singh (eds.), *The Weyward Sisters: Shakespeare and Feminist Politics*, Blackwell, 1994
A short and demanding section in the 'Acts of Resistance' chapter explores attitudes to the Witches in *Macbeth*.

William C Carroll (ed.), *Macbeth, Texts and Contexts*, Bedford St Martins, 1999
Contains documents from Shakespeare's time that relate to *Macbeth*, including material on the state of Scotland, sovereignty, witchcraft, theories of treason.

Linda Cookson and Brian Loughrey (eds.), *Critical Essays on Macbeth*, Longman, 1988
Collection of short essays on aspects of the play (e.g. treatment of evil, ceremony, the play as royalist propaganda).

Juliet Dusinberre, *Shakespeare and the Nature of Women*, Macmillan, 1975
An examination of changing attitudes to women, especially through Puritan thinking, and the ways the stage expressed popular controversies.

Terry Eagleton, *William Shakespeare*, Blackwell, 1986
Includes a short essay on *Macbeth* that exemplifies modern, radical perspectives. It sees the Witches subverting the social order, highlighting limitations of manhood, ambition, kingship.

Northrop Frye, *Fools of Time*, University of Toronto Press, 1967
Surveys the nature of tragedy from the Greeks through Seneca to the Elizabethans. Divides Shakespearean tragedy into three categories and considers *Macbeth* as a 'tragedy of order'. Stimulating ideas and comparisons, rather than detailed analysis of particular plays.

R B Heilman (ed.), *Shakespeare: The Tragedies, Twentieth Century Views*, Spectrum, 1984
Includes two essays on *Macbeth*. 'The Murderer as Victim' by E A J Honigman explores the various responses to the hero that complicate his status as a hated criminal. 'On Macbeth' by N Rabkin argues in a post-Freudian way that Macbeth is motivated more by a type of parricide (father-killing) than by ambition.

Russell Jackson (ed.), *Shakespeare on Film*, Cambridge University Press, 2000
Excellent guide with compact analyses of versions of the play by Welles, Kurosawa and Polanski in the essays by J. Lawrence Gunter, '*Hamlet*, *Macbeth*, and *King Lear* on film', and by Pamela Mason, 'Orson Welles and filmed Shakespeare'.

Frank Kermode, *Shakespeare's Language*, Allen Lane, 2000
A detailed examination of how Shakespeare's language changed during his playwriting career. Very useful chapter on *Macbeth*.

Victor Kiernan, *Eight Tragedies of Shakespeare: A Marxist Study*, Verso, 1996
Interprets the play in the political context of social change from feudalism to capitalism. Includes speculation about Shakespeare's changing attitudes.

Bernice Kliman, *Shakespeare in Performance: Macbeth*, Manchester University Press, 1992
Valuable analysis of performances on stage, film and TV. Selective treatment of twentieth-century interpretations, with detailed focus on film versions by Welles, Nunn and Polanski.

G Wilson Knight, *The Wheel of Fire: Interpretations of Shakespearean Tragedy*, Methuen, 1930
Examines symbols and images which Knight claims form unified patterns in Shakespeare's plays. He sees *Macbeth* as a 'vision of evil'.

L C Knights, *Explorations*, London, Chatto & Windus, 1946
Includes his essay 'How Many Children Had Lady Macbeth?', which mocks a character approach to the play.

Jan Kott, *Shakespeare Our Contemporary*, Methuen, 1965
An influential political reading of Shakespeare's plays which argues that Macbeth's murders reflect the horrors of twentieth-century society.

K Muir (ed.), *Aspects of Macbeth*, Cambridge University Press, 1977
A collection of essays, including R B Heilman's 'The Criminal as Tragic Hero', which begins with the premise that the play is unusual in that the hero is 'contracting' rather than enlarging spiritually.

Marvin Rosenberg, *The Masks of Macbeth*, University of California, 1978
Extremely thorough scene-by-scene account of the play with illustration and analysis from performances.

A R Rossiter, *Angel with Horns*, Longman, 1961
Avoids interpreting the play in terms of character and concentrates on its poetic qualities, atmosphere and the nature of evil.

Wilbur Sanders, *The Dramatist and the Received Idea*, Cambridge University Press, 1968
Includes two chapters on *Macbeth*, seeing it as a study of fear and an exploration of the nature of evil.

Alan Sinfield (ed.), *New Casebooks: Macbeth*, Macmillan, 1992
A collection of new critical approaches to *Macbeth*. The essays include feminist, political, psychoanalytical, structuralist and postmodern perspectives on the play.

Robert Smallwood (ed.), *Players of Shakespeare: Vol. 4*, Cambridge University Press, 1998
Includes an article by Derek Jacobi explaining his approach, speech by speech, to playing Macbeth for the Royal Shakespeare Company in 1993.

Caroline Spurgeon, *Shakespeare's Imagery and What it Tells Us*, Cambridge University Press, 1935
The first major study of imagery in the plays. Spurgeon's identification of image-clusters as a dominant feature of the plays has influenced all later studies.

John Wain (ed.), *Shakespeare: Macbeth, a Casebook*, Macmillan, 1968
A selection of influential essays written between 1751 and 1966.

Glynne Wickham, 'Hell Castle and its Door-keeper', *Shakespeare Survey 19*, Cambridge University Press, 1965
Examines the medieval mystery play *The Harrowing of Hell* and Shakespeare's use of it in the Porter scene, the role of Macduff and the ending of the play.

Films

Macbeth (USA, 1948) Director: Orson Welles. Orson Welles (Macbeth).
Welles describes his film as 'a violently sketched charcoal drawing of a great play'. Full of unusual features, it shows Macbeth drunk much of the time, Lady Macbeth talking to Macduff's son just before he is killed, and a 'Holy Father' who leads Malcolm's invading army against Macbeth.

Throne of Blood (Japan, 1957) Director: Akira Kurosawa. Toshiro Mifune (Macbeth/Washizu).
The Japanese dialogue is sparse, but the imagery, pace and atmosphere of the film thrillingly evoke the tensions and horror of Shakespeare's imaginative vision. Generally judged as a highly successful transformation of the play into film.

Macbeth (UK, 1971) Director: Roman Polanski. Jon Finch (Macbeth).
Notorious for its realistic on-screen portrayal of the play's offstage deaths, particularly the murder of Duncan and the savage slaughter at Macduff's castle. Polanski turns Ross into a political opportunist who appears as the Third Murderer, and who leaves the gates of Macduff's castle open for the killers to enter.

Macbeth (Thames TV, UK, 1978) Director: Trevor Nunn. Ian McKellen (Macbeth).
A television version of Trevor Nunn's highly acclaimed stage production at Stratford's Other Place in 1976. The tightly focused close-ups of faces convey the intensity of the characters' emotions and create a claustrophobic, anxiety-laden atmosphere.

Macbeth (BBC/Time-Life, UK, 1983) Director: Jack Gold. Nicol Williamson (Macbeth).
Part of the BBC's television series of all Shakespeare's plays. Williamson's voice becomes more rasping as evil takes hold on Macbeth.

Audio books

Major versions are easily obtainable in the series by Naxos, Arkangel, HarperCollins and BBC Radio Collection.

Macbeth on the Web

If you type 'Macbeth Shakespeare' into your search engine, it may find over 100,000 items. Because websites are of wildly varying quality, and rapidly disappear or are created, no recommendation can safely be made. But if you have time to browse you may find much of interest.